CILGERR...
ST DOGM...

PENTRE IFAN BURIAL CHAMBER
CARREG COETAN ARTHUR
BURIAL CHAMBER

John B. Hilling

Contents

Edited by Diane M. Williams BA, MA, PhD
Design by Staziker Jones

First Published 1992; Second Edition (Revised) 2000

Cadw: Welsh Historic Monuments (Crown Copyright),
Crown Building, Cathays Park, Cardiff, CF10 3NQ.

Printed in Great Britain by South Western Printers

ISBN 1 85760 116 5

The impressive remains of Pentre Ifan burial chamber have long attracted artistic and antiquarian interest. This is perhaps the most famous view, painted by Richard Tongue of Bath in 1835, and noted for combining 'near-accuracy with romantic art' (Society of Antiquaries).

A HISTORY OF CILGERRAN CASTLE

'AN ORNATE CASTLE OF MORTAR AND STONES'

Described in the thirteenth-century *Chronicle of the Princes* as 'an ornate castle of mortar and stones', Cilgerran remains one of the most picturesquely sited monuments in Wales. It lies a few miles south-east of Cardigan, perched high up on a rocky promontory overlooking the river Teifi. The rugged spur on which the castle stands is almost impregnable from the north, having been shaped on one side by the Teifi, which here flows in a deep gorge, and on the other by the Plysgog, a fast-flowing stream which tumbles down from the hills in a steep-sided valley. The site is near the tidal limit of the river, so that in the past it was accessible to sea-going ships.

These two principal features of Cilgerran — a dominating physical position and its strategic location — made it an obvious choice for the Anglo-Normans when, having advanced northwards, they decided to erect a stronghold from which to control their newly acquired lands. Yet, despite the obvious advantages, the castle was never an easy site to retain. In the century and a half following the first coming of the Norman invaders to the Teifi valley, Cilgerran was lost and rewon many times.

The entry for the year 1223 in the thirteenth-century Brut y Tywysogyon *(Chronicle of the Princes) describes Cilgerran as 'an ornate castle of mortar and stones' (National Library of Wales, Peniarth Ms. 20, p. 251).*

THE NORMAN ADVANCE: 1081–1135

A silver penny of William the Conqueror. King William (1066–87) claimed overlordship of Wales, including Deheubarth, and in 1081 he travelled to St Davids — ostensibly on pilgrimage, but in reality it was perhaps a show of strength (National Museums & Galleries of Wales).

On the eve of the Norman invasion, Cilgerran lay in the old Welsh *commote* of Is Cuch, which itself comprised that half of the *cantref* (or hundred) of Emlyn lying to the west of the Cuch. In turn, Emlyn was part of the kingdom of Deheubarth, which at that time included the whole of modern south-west Wales. And during the later part of the eleventh century, this ancient kingdom was to have its military and political power restored by the great Rhys ap Tewdwr (d. 1093).

William the Conqueror (1066–87) soon claimed overlordship of the region, and in 1081 he made an expedition to St Davids described in the Welsh *Chronicle of the Princes* (*Brut y Tywysogyon*) as 'a pilgrimage to offer prayers', but which in reality may have been a show of strength. For whatever reason, it appears that Rhys met the Conqueror during this royal expedition. They struck an agreement, whereby Rhys paid the king £40 a year as a fee for his continued rule of southern Wales. Despite the turbulent politics of the time, the good relationship lasted until William's death in 1087, but thereafter pressure began to build. Soon Rhys ap Tewdwr was being attacked both by fellow Welsh princes and by Norman freebooters. By 1091 his authority in Deheubarth was under serious threat. Only after the defeat of his distant kinsman, Gruffudd ap Maredudd, in a battle at Llandudoch (St Dogmaels) was his position once more assured. In the event, two years

Cilgerran Castle remains one of the most picturesquely sited monuments in Wales, perched high above the river Teifi atop a rocky promontory. It was this dominating physical position and strategic location that attracted the first Anglo-Norman castle-builders (Skyscan Balloon Photography, for Cadw: Welsh Historic Monuments).

NEST: THE 'HELEN OF WALES'

Nest, the daughter of Rhys ap Tewdwr (d. 1093) and wife of Gerald of Windsor, was renowned for her beauty. As a princess of Deheubarth she was a notable 'catch' for Gerald in his bid to establish himself more firmly in Pembrokeshire. There were three sons from the union and a daughter, Angharad, who became, in turn, the mother of Gerald of Wales.

The abduction of Nest in 1109 from the castle of Cenarth Bychan by her second-cousin, Owain ap Cadwgan, is fully documented in the medieval *Chronicle of the Princes (Brut y Tywysogyon)*. According to the chronicle, when 'Owain had heard that Nest was in the castle, he went with but a few men in his company to visit her as a kinswoman. And after that he came of a night to the castle and but few men with him, about fourteen, unknown to the keepers of the castle. And then he came to the chamber in which Gerald and Nest were sleeping. And they raised a shout around and about the chamber in which Gerald was, and kindled tapers and set fire to the buildings to burn them. And when he heard the shout, Gerald awoke, not knowing what to do. And then Nest said to him, "Go not out to the door, for thine enemies await thee, but follow me".

And that he did. And she led him to the privy which adjoined the chamber. And there, as is said, he escaped by the way of the privy hole. And when Nest knew that he had escaped, she cried out from within and said to the men who were outside, "Why do you cry out in vain? He whom you seek is not here. He has escaped". And when they did not find him, they seized Nest and her two sons and her daughter and another son of his by a concubine, and they sacked and plundered the castle'.

It was not the first, nor the last, of Nest's amorous adventures. She is reputed to have told Owain: 'If thou wouldst have me faithful to thee and keep me with thee, have my children escorted to their father'. It is impossible to know, at this distance of time, whether this was guile or a desire to stay with Owain. Nest became the mistress of a number of lovers, including King Henry I, earning herself notoriety as the 'Helen of Wales'.

A full account of the abduction of Nest from the castle at Cenarth Bychan appears in Brut y Tywysogyon, part of which is shown on this page from the book (National Library of Wales, Peniarth Ms. 20).

Princess Nest achieved some notoriety as a mistress to many lovers — including King Henry I (1100–35) — earning for herself the sobriquet 'Helen of Wales' (British Library, Additional Ms. 10292, f. 21v).

later Rhys himself was killed near Brecon while supporting a neighbouring Welsh prince against the advancing Normans.

Rhys's death served almost as a signal to the Normans. Within a matter of months Roger of Montgomery, earl of Shrewsbury (d. 1094), had moved from his base in the Severn valley and overrun Ceredigion, reaching the mouth of the Teifi where he commenced building a castle at Cardigan. From there he moved on southwards, establishing a castle and lordship at Pembroke. At the same time, a seaborne invasion gave the Normans footholds around the coastal estuaries, with another castle quickly thrown up at Rhyd y Gors near Carmarthen. As in the north, it must have seemed that the southern half of Wales had been all but conquered by the invaders. But in fact the Normans had overreached themselves. Between 1094 and 1098, revolts broke out in all parts of Wales, and the Normans were soon in retreat. They were forced to give up all their outposts in the south-west except Pembroke.

The inability of the Welsh princes to unseat the Normans from Pembroke was eventually to be their undoing, and gradually the Norman lords were able to reconquer parts of Deheubarth. About 1102, the custody of Pembroke Castle was given to Gerald of Windsor, a Norman adventurer who had earlier defended the castle during the Welsh revolt of 1096. Shortly after receiving Pembroke, he set about building a second castle at Carew on land which had come to him as a dowry when he married Nest, the beautiful daughter of Rhys ap Tewdwr. Not content with two castles, and seeking more land, Gerald advanced northwards over Mynydd Preseli and set about building a third castle, which in 1108 'he fortified with a ditch and a wall'. The place he chose was called Cenarth Bychan, situated in the western part of Emlyn. In the event, the establishment of this castle was to represent the origins of the lordship of Cilgerran.

The location of Cenarth Bychan is not known with any degree of certainty, though it is probably the same as Cilgerran. The site is likely to have been reasonably close to Cenarth Mawr, the original centre of Emlyn, while at the same time accessible from the sea. Gerald, however, had barely had time to settle in his new fortification when it was attacked. In 1109, Owain ap Cadwgan (d. 1116) of Powys broke into the stronghold and abducted — perhaps

Above: *The earliest earth-and-timber fortification at Cilgerran is likely to have taken the form of a 'ringwork'. This reconstruction drawing — based on archaeological excavations in 1960–61 — shows the ringwork known as Castle Tower at Penmaen, on the Gower peninsula. Here, the main strongpoint of the castle is the gate-tower and it is possible that the twelfth-century defences at Cilgerran took a similar form (Illustration by Terry Ball, 1987).*

Right: *A detail from* Brut y Tywysogyon *that records the construction of Cenarth Bychan by Gerald of Windsor, which in 1108 'he fortified with a ditch and a wall' (National Library of Wales, Peniarth Ms. 20).*

not unwillingly — Gerald's wife, Nest, while Gerald himself was forced to make an undignified escape down a latrine shaft.

Presumably Gerald eventually returned to Cenarth Bychan — although there are no further records of a castle of that name — for this was a period during which the Normans were reasserting their hold on south-western Wales. In 1110, a new castle was built at Cardigan by Gilbert fitz Richard (d. 1114–17), and during the next few years both St Dogmaels Abbey and Cardigan Priory were founded. During the same period, Flemish settlers were deliberately introduced to south-west Wales by King Henry I (1100–35). At the expense of the native inhabitants, groups of Flemings were to occupy the area between the Cleddau rivers and Mynydd Preseli.

The fourteenth-century tomb effigy of Rhys ap Gruffudd (d. 1197) — the Lord Rhys — in the cathedral church at St Davids. The Lord Rhys was successful in reasserting Welsh authority in south-west Wales after decades of Norman advance. In 1165 he captured Cilgerran, held for over thirty years until his death in 1197.

By 1172, King Henry II (1154–89), seen here in a contemporary manuscript, had struck an accord with the Lord Rhys, and eventually made him 'justice on his behalf in all Deheubarth' (National Library of Ireland, Ms. 700).

STEMMING THE TIDE: WELSH RESURGENCE 1136–1222

The Norman ascendancy in the Teifi valley was short lived and, for a while at least, the tide was stemmed if not turned. In 1136, a combined Norman and Flemish army was decisively defeated at the battle of Crug Mawr, north of the Teifi near Cardigan, and Gerald of Windsor's son was killed. Two years later, St Dogmaels Abbey was raided by marauding Vikings, and Norman authority south of the Teifi in Cilgerran and Cemais was called into question. Gradually the Welsh princes reasserted their rule in a widening area of Deheubarth.

In 1155, the young Rhys ap Gruffudd (d. 1197), grandson of Rhys ap Tewdwr, became the undisputed ruler of Deheubarth. After an initial show of defiance he submitted to the overlordship of Henry II (1154–89) and was deprived of Ceredigion for his pains. Rhys bided his time. When, in 1165, Henry tried once again to crush the Welsh, Rhys — along with Owain Gwynedd (d. 1170) in the north — took up arms and the king returned to England empty handed. Rhys recaptured Cardigan and Cilgerran, and seized the districts of Ceredigion and Emlyn. According to the Welsh chronicles, Rhys found Robert fitz Stephen, the son of Nest, at Cilgerran and so he imprisoned him. In the following year, Normans from Pembroke (together with Flemings) twice laid siege to Cilgerran Castle. According to the *Chronicle of the Princes*, they suffered heavy losses but were still unable to take the fortress.

When next the king travelled to Wales his policy towards Rhys had changed considerably. The two men met in the forest of Dean, and again at Pembroke in 1171 and at Laugharne in 1172. At these meetings a new accord was struck. The king made the Welsh prince 'justice on his behalf in all Deheubarth', and in return Rhys supported the king in his later campaigns. In 1176, the Lord Rhys — as he is generally known — held a great assembly of musicians and poets at Cardigan Castle. This festival of music and poetry was perhaps the forerunner of the modern eisteddfod with competitors coming from all parts of Wales, as well as other countries.

By the time of Henry II's death in 1189, Rhys's position as ruler of the Deheubarth heartlands was secure. Subsequently, he sought to extend his control further, attacking those areas where the Norman grip remained tight. In this, he and his sons were partly successful, capturing or besieging many Norman strongholds as far afield as Wiston, Swansea, and Painscastle. Rhys built a new castle at Rhayader, and rebuilt anew the Norman stronghold at Kidwelly. And to the west, in 1191, he captured Nevern Castle during a sweep across Cemais to ensure a buffer zone between Emlyn and anglicized Pembroke.

Rhys ap Gruffudd, 'the shield and strength of the South', died in 1197. With his death Deheubarth entered into a dark period marked by family feuds and petty jealousies. Rhys was succeeded by his son Gruffudd (d. 1201) who, in turn, was seized by another son, Maelgwn (d. 1231), and handed over to the English. The following year Gruffudd was released and in 1198 he regained Cilgerran. His possession of Cilgerran and Emlyn was weakened, however, when his brother Maelgwn sold Cardigan Castle to King John (1199–1216) for 200 marks (£133 6s. 8d.) in return for royal protection. Gruffudd's position was further weakened by the building of a new Anglo-Norman castle at Newport, replacing the older stronghold at Nevern.

Then, in 1204, the 'dashing and brilliant' William Marshal the elder (d. 1219), earl of Pembroke, marched to Cilgerran with a large

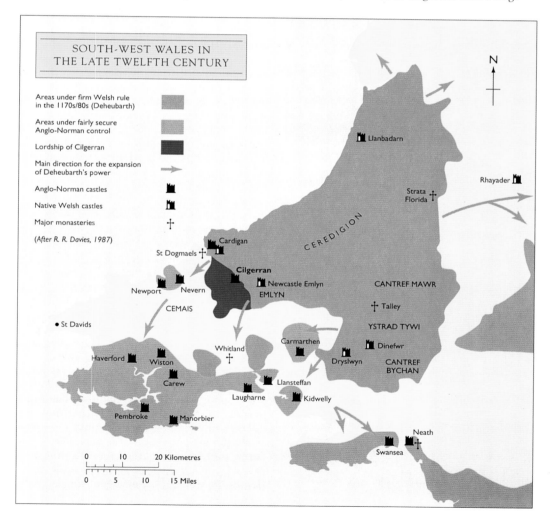

SOUTH-WEST WALES IN THE LATE TWELFTH CENTURY

Areas under firm Welsh rule in the 1170s/80s (Deheubarth)

Areas under fairly secure Anglo-Norman control

Lordship of Cilgerran

Main direction for the expansion of Deheubarth's power

Anglo-Norman castles

Native Welsh castles

Major monasteries

(After R. R. Davies, 1987)

N

Llanbadarn

Rhayader

Strata Florida

CEREDIGION

Cardigan

St Dogmaels

Cilgerran

Newcastle Emlyn

CANTREF MAWR

Newport   Nevern

EMLYN

Talley

CEMAIS

• St Davids

YSTRAD TYWI

Whitland   Carmarthen   Dinefwr

Haverford   Wiston   Dryslwyn   CANTREF BYCHAN

Carew   Llansteffan

Laugharne   Kidwelly

Pembroke   Manorbier

Neath

0   10   20 Kilometres

Swansea

0   5   10   15 Miles

army. With astonishing speed, he captured the castle even before the guards in the Welsh garrison could arm themselves. And yet Earl William's hold on Cilgerran was comparatively short lived. For in 1215, in a remarkable and enterprising move, Prince Llywelyn ab Iorwerth (d. 1240) of Gwynedd seized an opportunity to unite the Deheubarth princelings. Together, in a single sweeping campaign, they recovered much of south-west Wales, taking not only Cilgerran, but also the castles of Cardigan and Newport. By 1218, all the lordships of the south-west, apart from Pembroke, were held by Llywelyn or his Deheubarth allies.

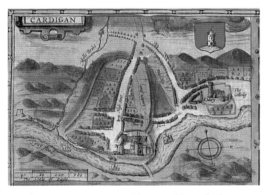

Above: *Although the town, castle and priory at Cardigan were established by the Normans, they enjoyed several decades of Welsh patronage under the Lord Rhys in the second half of the twelfth century. But this was not to last, for by the middle of the thirteenth century, Cardigan served as a major royal centre in west Wales. This, the earliest known plan of the town by John Speed, dates from 1610 (National Library of Wales).*

Left: *This tomb effigy in Temple Church, City of London represents William Marshal the elder (d. 1219), who captured the castle of Cilgerran from the Welsh with remarkable speed in 1204.*

CILGERRAN UNDER THE MARSHAL AND HASTINGS FAMILIES

Meanwhile, the Marshals had been strengthening their power bases in both the southern March and in Ireland. William the younger (d. 1231) was determined to recover his father's position in west Wales, and in 1223 he landed at St Davids with an army brought from across the water. Marching on Cardigan and Cilgerran, he expelled the Welsh allies and recaptured both castles. Thereafter, although Cardigan was taken once more by Prince Llywelyn, Cilgerran never again fell to the Welsh.

Following William the younger's death, each of his four brothers in turn became earl of Pembroke. All of them had died by 1245, and none had produced a male heir. Twelve years later, in 1257, Cilgerran's defences were to be severely tested. The Gwynedd prince, Llywelyn ap Gruffudd (d. 1282), gained possession of nearby Cemais, destroying Newport Castle in the process. In the following year an alliance of Welsh princes defeated the English in a fierce battle fought near Cilgerran. According to the Welsh annals, 'the English were put to flight, leaving the corpses of the dead with their armed horses behind them'. The castle was attacked and suffered much damage but managed to survive the onslaught.

During the interim, the extensive Pembroke estates had been divided among the five surviving Marshal sisters. The lordship of Cilgerran passed to Eva, widow of William de Braose (d. 1230) of Abergavenny. Her daughter, another Eva, married William Cantilupe (d. 1254) and thus, for a time, the lordship of Cilgerran severed its connection with the earldom of Pembroke. On William Cantilupe's death, the lordship passed to his son, George, who was just two years old. George died in 1273, and thereafter Cilgerran went to his sister Joan's son, John de Hastings (d. 1313), who was also a minor. The Hastings family continued to hold both the lordships of Cilgerran and Abergavenny for more than a century.

We should, however, bear in mind that during the minorities of the heirs, Cilgerran was in the hands of the Crown. There are a few records, for example, of stewards acting on

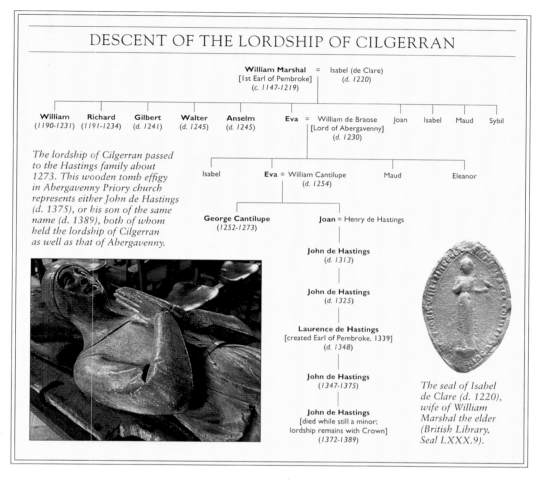

DESCENT OF THE LORDSHIP OF CILGERRAN

William Marshal = Isabel (de Clare)
[1st Earl of Pembroke]   (d. 1220)
(c. 1147-1219)

William (1190-1231) · Richard (1191-1234) · Gilbert (d. 1241) · Walter (d. 1245) · Anselm (d. 1245) · Eva = William de Braose [Lord of Abergavenny] (d. 1230) · Joan · Isabel · Maud · Sybil

The lordship of Cilgerran passed to the Hastings family about 1273. This wooden tomb effigy in Abergavenny Priory church represents either John de Hastings (d. 1375), or his son of the same name (d. 1389), both of whom held the lordship of Cilgerran as well as that of Abergavenny.

Isabel · Eva = William Cantilupe (d. 1254) · Maud · Eleanor

George Cantilupe (1252-1273)

Joan = Henry de Hastings

John de Hastings (d. 1313)

John de Hastings (d. 1325)

Laurence de Hastings [created Earl of Pembroke, 1339] (d. 1348)

John de Hastings (1347-1375)

John de Hastings [died while still a minor; lordship remains with Crown] (1372-1389)

The seal of Isabel de Clare (d. 1220), wife of William Marshal the elder (British Library, Seal LXXX.9).

behalf of the Lord Edward — the future King Edward I (1272–1307) — in the lordship. There is no direct evidence for any concern with the castle buildings at this time, but such a lack of interest in what remained an unsettled period would be somewhat surprising. Certainly, in the 1260s and 1270s, Prince Llywelyn ('the Last') of Gwynedd was at the peak of his power. His political and military superiority meant that the lordships of the southern March were subject to constant pressure.

The apparent lack of concern may be partly explained by the fact that, at first, Maredudd ap Rhys (d. 1271), grandson of the Lord Rhys and builder of the nearby castle in Emlyn (Newcastle Emlyn) about 1240, was more an ally of the Valence earls of Pembroke than of Prince Llywelyn. Yet by 1270 Maredudd had been persuaded to give his allegiance to Llywelyn,

and the security of the lordship of Cilgerran must have begun to look shaky indeed.

There are some telling insights into the condition of the castle in 1275. In that year, an inquisition taken before the king's bailiff suggests that, during Nicholas fitz Martin's recent custody, damage done to towers, houses and other buildings at the site would take at least 100 marks (£66) to repair. Two years later, during the first war of Welsh independence, Ceredigion was easily overrun by the forces of King Edward I (1272–1307). Cilgerran itself appears to have been bypassed.

Any major building work which may have been carried out after the 1275 inquisition was probably limited to the curtain walls, for within fifty years the castle was again unusable. In 1326, it was said to be 'worth nothing' (in rent) because it lay 'in ruins'. Indeed, it was not until the latter years of the fourteenth century that external events made it necessary to repair the stronghold. In 1369, England's war with France had been resumed and in 1372 John de Hastings (d. 1375), now earl of Pembroke as well as lord of Cilgerran, was sent with the fleet to reinforce the English position in Aquitaine. He was defeated off the coast of La Rochelle. This led to fears of a retaliatory invasion of England and a Welsh rising under Owain Lawgoch (d. 1378). By 1377 a French landing in Pembrokeshire appeared imminent, and Edward III (1327–77) ordered Cilgerran and Pembroke — now in his hands due to the minority of the last John de Hastings — to be repaired and fortified. But the blow fell elsewhere and Cilgerran resumed its peaceful existence.

In 1414 Henry V (1413–22) granted Cilgerran and Pembroke to his youngest brother, Humphrey, who in the following year was created duke of Gloucester (d. 1447). Duke Humphrey is shown in this manuscript illustration with his wife, Eleanor of Cobham (British Library, Nero Ms. D VII, f. 154).

LATER HISTORY OF THE CASTLE

The last John de Hastings died in 1389 whilst still a minor, and as a result the lordship of Cilgerran remained with the Crown. In the following year, we learn of further very minor repairs to the castle costing 6s. 6d. The expenditure shows that maintenance continued in this period. A few years later, about 1405, at the height of the Owain Glyn Dŵr uprising, Cilgerran may have been held by the rebel forces. A subsequent report mentions damage done to the castle.

Thereafter little is heard of Cilgerran Castle. The lordship continued to be associated with the earldom of Pembroke and was granted by the Crown to its chief supporters, notably Humphrey, duke of Gloucester (d. 1447), from 1414 to 1447, and Jasper Tudor (d. 1495) from 1452 to 1461 and 1485 to 1495. The custody of the castle was granted by Henry VII (1485–1509) to William Vaughan, apparently as a reward for sheltering him and his uncle, Jasper Tudor, before they were forced to flee to France by Edward IV (d. 1483). In 1536–43, the Act of Union swept away the Marcher lordships and Cilgerran became part of the newly created county of Pembrokeshire.

During the Civil War of 1642–48 successive waves of Royalist and Parliamentary forces swept across Pembrokeshire, and bloody

Between 1452 and 1461, the earldom of Pembroke, together with the lordship of Cilgerran, was held by Jasper Tudor (d. 1495). Earl Jasper — the reverse of whose great seal is shown here — held Cilgerran for a second time between 1485 and 1495, following the accession of his nephew, King Henry VII (1485–1509) (British Library).

battles were fought at nearby Cardigan and Newcastle Emlyn in 1645. It seems unlikely that Cilgerran would have been unaffected by the war, yet there are no records of its involvement nor of any attempts to fortify the by then ancient stronghold.

By 1685 the castle had passed to the Pryse family of Gogerddan. A century later it was a Romantic ruin which was beginning to be visited by artists such as Richard Wilson (1714–82) and J. M. W. Turner (1775–1851).

The castle was treated with scant respect in the nineteenth century and the dry ditch of the bailey was converted into the village pound. As a result of the slate quarrying which was carried on around the castle, an even worse fate was to befall the curtain wall of the bailey. In 1863 a large stretch of it fell down 'with a tremendous crash'. In 1938, Mrs Colby acquired the castle from Sir Lewes Pryse for the National Trust. Five years later, care of the ruins was handed over to the State. They are now maintained by Cadw: Welsh Historic Monuments.

By the mid-eighteenth century, Cilgerran had become a Romantic ruin, to be visited and painted by numerous artists and topographical illustrators. This engraving, by S. H. Grimm, appeared in Henry Wyndham's A Tour Through Monmouthshire and South Wales, *second edition, 1781 (National Library of Wales).*

J. M. W. Turner (1775–1851) made several studies of Cilgerran and the site seems to have exerted a special fascination on him. This worked-up study comes from his Hereford Court sketchbook which documents his 1798 tour of Wales (Turner Bequest, Tate Gallery BM: TB XXXVIII, f. 100).

THE CONSTRUCTION AND PLANNING OF CILGERRAN CASTLE

THE TWELFTH CENTURY

Very little of the castle which can be seen today dates from the twelfth century. The first stronghold, whether built by Gerald of Windsor in 1108, or somewhat later, may well have been in the form known as a 'ringwork'. By constructing such a castle at the confluence of the Teifi and Plysgog, its builder was able to take advantage of the natural defences on the north-east and north-west sides where the scarp slopes steeply down to the river and its tributary. The exposed southern side was probably defended by the crescent-shaped, rock-cut ditch which survives across the neck of the spur. In which case, the basic shape of the later stone castle was formed by this ditch, and it now represents all that remains of the earliest fortification on the site.

The later stone inner ward may, therefore, mark the inner bailey of the original ringwork. On the inside of the ringwork ditch, there would probably have been an artificial bank surmounted by a timber palisade. At some point around the circuit of the ringwork there would almost certainly have been a strongpoint. At other ringwork castles, such strongpoints took the form of a gate-tower, and at Cilgerran such a structure could have been located on the small area of flat rock between the later gatehouse and the west tower.

As time went by, the defences and some of the internal wooden buildings were probably rebuilt in stone. Indeed, the rock on which the castle stands is of a slatey nature, and its regular and close cleavage planes make it easy to split into thin slabs, ideal for dry-stone walling. It seems possible, therefore, that stone was used in various aspects of the construction at quite an early date. Two remnants of such early masonry walls, which were originally bedded in clay rather than mortar, survive near the inner gatehouse, and at the northern edge of the inner ward. They probably belong to one of the later stages of the ringwork castle, as possibly does the remnant of apparently early walling embedded in the cross-curtain wall between the east and west towers (p. 21).

THE EARLY THIRTEENTH CENTURY

The almost total absence of dressed stone in the castle means that architectural detail is scarce, and it is therefore difficult to date the different parts of the building on stylistic grounds. However, a major rebuilding of the castle in stone was fortunately recorded in the *Chronicle of the Princes (Brut y Tywysogyon)*. From one version of the chronicle we learn that in 1223 William Marshal (the younger) began to build 'an ornate castle of mortar and stones', and that soon after commencing the work he was called away to meet the king, sailing 'in a ship to England, after leaving all his host at Cilgerran to hold the work he had begun, and bidding them give support where they should see peril'.

As eventually completed, the plan of the inner ward at Cilgerran is basically similar to that of Pembroke Castle, built about twenty years earlier by William Marshal the elder. At Pembroke, the end of a promontory is also cut off by a curved cross-curtain wall following the line of an earlier ditch. Moreover, both inner wards have gatehouses towards the left-hand side and round towers towards the right-hand side (though it must be said this may be a feature of the natural topography at both sites).

The main difference in the two layouts is that Pembroke has an enormous round keep mid-way along, but set behind, the cross-curtain wall. Cilgerran does not have a keep, in the sense of an independent self-defensible residential tower, but it does have a second round tower set at a mid-point on the cross-curtain wall.

Both of the Cilgerran round towers have an internal diameter of twenty-two feet (6.4m). They were built on a massive scale, reminiscent of the early thirteenth-century Anglo-Norman round keeps at Pembroke, Skenfrith and Tretower, or the Welsh castle at Dinefwr. Architecturally, the Cilgerran towers are similar to the Pembroke keep in their degree

A SUGGESTED SEQUENCE OF CONSTRUCTION

THE TWELFTH-CENTURY CASTLE

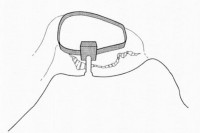

In the absence of firm archaeological evidence, this phase must be considered entirely conjectural. It seems probable that the earliest Norman stronghold took the form of a 'ringwork', which is likely to have had a strongpoint in the form of a gate-tower.

THIRTEENTH CENTURY: PERIOD IA (1223)

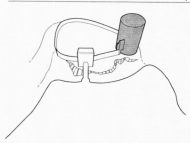

In 1223 William Marshal the younger began a major new stone castle at Cilgerran. It appears that the east tower was at first built independently of the west tower.

THIRTEENTH CENTURY: PERIOD IB

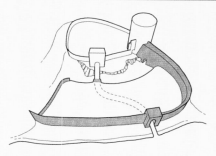

The initial stone defences of the outer ward, including the south outer gatehouse, were probably raised in the early thirteenth century, after the construction of the east tower.

THIRTEENTH CENTURY: PERIOD 2

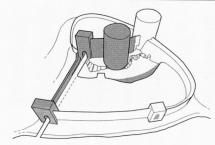

The west tower and inner gatehouse were the work of a later Marshal heir, perhaps Earl Gilbert (d. 1241).

LATER THIRTEENTH CENTURY

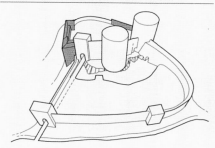

Further minor works appear to have been undertaken in the second half of the thirteenth century.

FOURTEENTH CENTURY

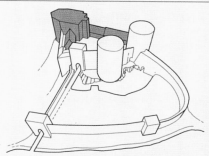

The last major works undertaken at the castle probably relate to the repair and refortification undertaken on the orders of King Edward III (1327–77) in the late 1370s.

Cilgerran is distinguished by its two massive round towers which straddle the line of the cross-curtain wall. Architecturally, they are reminiscent of the round keeps at a number of castles including Pembroke and Dinefwr, but at each of these sites the great towers are surrounded by a protective ring of curtain walls.

William Marshal the elder's great round keep at Pembroke was built soon after 1200–01, some twenty years before his sons were to emulate its size and form at Cilgerran.

Although much altered in later years, the massive round keep at Dinefwr bears comparison with Cilgerran and Pembroke and is thought to date from the early years of the thirteenth century.

of austerity. Each tower was large enough to serve as a residential keep. Moreover, both had fireplaces and some domestic windows. But there are a number of differences in detail which suggest that the plainer east tower — standing on the highest part of the inner ward — was the first to be built.

Indeed, when it was erected, a direct link to the future west tower had almost certainly not been envisaged. A vertical break in the masonry of the cross-curtain wall, together with a noticeable change in the direction of the curtain wall itself, confirms that all to the west of this break was built later. The vertical break itself may have been caused by the remnants of an earlier structure, perhaps lying at right angles to the later cross-curtain. Alternatively, the toothing on the outer face of the curtain at this point (p. 21), could mark the position of a barbican or outer defence.

Most of the cross-curtain wall, the west tower and the inner gatehouse are all of the same build and, therefore, of the same date. In practice, the west tower functioned as the keep, its main floor being reached by an external flight of stairs, as at Pembroke and elsewhere. Its position, astride the cross-curtain wall, seems to have been dictated by the existing shape of the rock-cut ditch over which it is partly built. If the tower had been set behind the cross-curtain wall, as at Pembroke, then the wall would have needed to follow the curve of the ditch and this would have made it impossible to defend the wall by enfilading fire from the east tower and inner gatehouse. The tower was therefore brought forward to the cross-curtain and in this position it acted as both keep and defensive wall tower.

There remains the question as to why Cilgerran should have needed two towers of such large proportions. A possible answer is that each tower was built for the same purpose, but at different times — perhaps by different people — in answer to changed circumstances. Indeed, it looks as though it was intended at first to build only the east tower.

The angle of the cross-curtain wall immediately adjacent to that tower is aligned with the flat rock floor between the west tower and the gatehouse. This suggests that, originally, it may have been intended to link the east tower directly to the putative earlier gatehouse, situated on this area of flat rock. The decision to construct a new gatehouse near the edge of the steep-sided Plysgog valley provided the opportunity to build the west tower in the vacated space. The tower would have been necessary to improve the protection of an otherwise long length of curving curtain wall.

In short, the evidence suggests that the 'ornate castle' of William Marshal the younger — mentioned in the *Chronicle of the Princes* as being built in 1223 — is perhaps represented by the east tower. The west tower may well have been built by one of his brothers somewhat later, possibly after 1231. A likely builder for this later work was Gilbert Marshal (d. 1241). He is known, for instance, to have carried out a vigorous building programme at one of his other castles, Chepstow. The need to strengthen Cilgerran may have been brought about by events which, in 1240, culminated in the reconstruction of the nearby castle at Cardigan for the king by Gilbert's younger brother, Walter (d. 1245).

A reconstruction of Cilgerran Castle as it may have appeared in the later Middle Ages, following the addition of the north tower in the last major phase of construction (Illustration by Chris Jones-Jenkins, 1992).

LATER ADDITIONS AND ALTERATIONS

There appears to have been a general rebuilding of the curtain walls of the inner ward overlooking the Teifi and Plysgog in the later part of the thirteenth century. They must have been built after 1275, for in that year an inquisition found the castle to be 'defective in towers and in all other buildings, as well as in walls and other things'.

The last major development of the castle included the construction of the north tower overlooking the Teifi. The tower is built across the broken end of the north-west curtain wall showing that it was added on later. The surviving detail suggests the fourteenth century, which accords with the order given by King Edward III in 1377 to repair the castle. The design of the door jambs to the domestic buildings erected along the north side of the inner ward is similar and indicates that these buildings date from much the same period. The lower doorway of the west tower is also similar, and confirms that the ground floor of this tower was altered in the fourteenth century.

A BIRD'S-EYE VIEW OF CILGERRAN CASTLE
FROM THE NORTH

1 Outer ward — *separated from the inner ward by a rock-cut ditch, it housed buildings associated with the utilitarian aspects of castle life (pp. 17–18).*

2 South outer gatehouse — *a simple but solid construction, it was presumably closed with large wooden gates. There was no portcullis, and the gate may have been superseded by the gatehouse known to have existed at a point near to the modern entrance to the castle (p. 17).*

3 Inner gatehouse — *originally three storeys high, the entrance passage was protected by a timber gate and two portcullises. The room above the gate-passage appears to have served as a small chapel (p. 18).*

4 West tower — *the principal residential tower in the castle which was originally entered at first-floor level by a timber staircase. There were large hooded fireplaces on both the first and second floors. There was a link to the east tower via the cross-curtain wall (pp. 18–20).*

5 East tower — *plainer than the west tower, with only one fireplace on the third floor. It was probably the first of the pair to be built and represents the core of the masonry castle begun by William Marshal the younger in 1223 (pp. 20–1).*

6 Latrines — *the end of the east curtain wall overlooks the precipitous side of the valley. From the wall-walk there was access to a pair of latrines, the shafts of which survive (p. 21).*

7 Domestic buildings — *low foundations survive against the rear defences and probably represent domestic buildings. One of these is likely to have served as a hall (pp. 22–3).*

8 North tower — *scant remains of the tower which overlooked a navigable stretch of the Teifi, and probably dates from the late fourteenth century (p. 22).*

9 Kitchen — *further domestic buildings line the north-west curtain and may have included a kitchen. The remains of a limekiln can also be seen (p. 23).*

(Illustration by Terry Ball)

A TOUR OF CILGERRAN CASTLE

The castle stands on a rocky promontory behind the village and is approached down a narrow street. The modern entrance lies at the south-west corner of the outer ward. Archaeological excavation in this area (just in front of the iron gates) indicates that there was a gateway, with a portcullis, in this position in medieval times. This tour first explores the outer ward of the castle and then proceeds through the inner gateway to the inner ward.

THE OUTER WARD

The gently sloping outer ward is separated from the inner ward by a rock-cut ditch, or dry moat, which may well date from the earliest ('ringwork') phase of the castle. The ditch was later revetted in stone on the outer face. At the furthest end of the ditch (to the right as you enter) there is a section of the massive curtain wall that originally enclosed the outer ward. You will just see the remains of the wall-walk near the top of this wall. The gateway below is a sally port which, when used in conjunction with the gate next to the east tower, allowed the

The two sombre round towers dominate any view of Cilgerran Castle, seen here separated from the outer ward by the substantial rock-cut ditch.

castle's defenders to 'sally forth', and to surprise attackers from behind. The curtain wall was considerably reduced in length in 1863 when 56 feet (17m) of it fell as a result of undermining from the adjacent slate quarry.

Glance up at the sombre round towers and notice how, on this side, there are no windows, but only carefully placed arrowslits in the walls overlooking the ditch. The west tower (left) is embellished with two thin string courses and has a slightly battered base. The top of the east tower (right) is marked by a series of rectangular drainage holes, each incorporating a slate channel.

Walk up to the very highest part of the outer ward to the remains of the south, or outer, gatehouse. The narrow lane beyond the gate occupies the

site of the outer ditch which has been filled in. The gatehouse is a fairly simple, but solid, affair. It was presumably closed off with large gates, but there is no evidence for a portcullis, which suggests that it belongs to an early phase of the stone castle. It may have been superseded later by the excavated outer gate (near the current entrance), which had the more advanced feature of a portcullis.

Nearby are low walls of other buildings. The long, rectangular building is divided into three rooms, one of which contains the base of a kiln or oven. Postholes in the outer walls show that the upper parts of the building were constructed in timber. From here, you should now walk down to the footbridge leading to the inner ward.

BRIDGE AND INNER GATEHOUSE

The rectangular inner gatehouse is reached by a modern bridge carried over the inner ditch on stone abutments which survive from a late medieval bridge. This bridge replaced a still earlier drawbridge. In order to make access to the gatehouse as difficult as possible, the rock-cut ditch was further deepened in the area beneath the drawbridge. The original entrance to the inner ward seems to have been slightly further east, probably on the flat rock platform between the west tower and the gatehouse. The site of its bridge is marked by a stone abutment on the opposite side of the ditch.

Before entering the gatehouse notice the squinch arrowslit in the corner between the tower and the cross-curtain wall. This was intended to provide covering fire for the gatehouse. At the top of the wall can be seen the remains of a corbelled parapet and, below this, three arrowslits in which an attempt has been made to use dressed stone to give them shape.

Only the inner arch of the gatehouse now remains, though it was originally three storeys high. The entrance passage was protected by a timber gate and two portcullises, lowered down from above in the vertical grooves which can be seen in the side walls. The room above the gate had a stone-vaulted ceiling. A small arched recess in one wall of this room was possibly used for a piscina (or basin) in which a priest could wash sacred vessels. This suggests that, besides housing the mechanism for lowering and raising the portcullises, the room may have been used as a chapel.

The remains of the inner gatehouse and adjacent curtain wall. To the right is the squinch arrowslit that would have provided covering fire for the gatehouse. Above the gate-passage can be seen the remains of a room which appears to have been a small chapel.

THE INNER WARD

The inner ward, or courtyard, is dominated by the two great round towers and linking cross-curtain wall, all of which date from the early thirteenth century. Both towers are four storeys high and were built with massively thick walls on the outer sides, away from the courtyard, where an attack was most likely.

The West Tower

The west tower was the principal residential tower and was originally entered at first-floor level. The entrance doorway was immediately above the existing (later) entrance, and was reached by an external wooden stair. The break in the stonework above the doorway suggests that it was protected from the weather by a gabled porch.

The present ground-floor doorway is a later adaptation, probably inserted in the fourteenth century, when the room was divided into two by building an octagonal pier in the centre and adding a cross-wall. Originally the ground floor was accessible only from the room above, probably by a trapdoor, and was gloomily lit by the single high-level shaft in the outer wall.

The spiral stairs leading to the first floor were inserted in the thickness of the wall at the same time as the ground-floor entrance was constructed. The present first-floor landing

A general view across the inner ward, looking towards the east tower. The west tower is to the right.

crosses in front of the earlier entrance, which was either blocked or converted into a window. The first-floor room has a hooded fireplace and was originally lit by a flat-headed window overlooking the courtyard.

Another spiral stairway leads up to the second floor. Steps off the quarter landing give access to the wall-passage that led to the inner gatehouse. The passage has alcoves on each side, those on the outer side being pierced by arrowslits. Originally, there was a wall-walk, or even a second passage, situated above

and accessible from the third floor of the tower.

You should now return to the tower and cross the modern footbridge to the opposite side. From the footbridge the positions of all the upper floors can be easily made out by the large beam-holes formed in the walls to take the massive timber floor beams. The second-floor room has a hooded fireplace similar to the one below. The single-light window was positioned above the entrance to allow visitors on the outer staircase to be scrutinized before entering.

The first-floor chamber in the west tower was heated by means of a large hooded fireplace, as befitted the main residential accommodation in the castle.

Three arrowslits can be seen in this room. They have horizontal sighting grooves, but are otherwise of a rather crude design with very narrow embrasures. No recesses were provided — as in later arrowslits at other castles — for the archer to stand in. Consequently, he had to position himself well back, thus reducing the field of fire. It would seem that these openings would have provided a less than effective means of defence.

The doorway at the end of the footbridge opens on to the wall-walk above the central section of the cross-curtain wall. This leads to the east tower.

The East Tower

The wall-walk has a curious twist and change of level in it just before reaching the east tower. This is because the east tower was built first, and at the time of its construction no allowance appears to have been made for a possible connection with a future west tower (pp. 18–20).

The east tower and its curtain wall, although basically similar to the west tower complex, were even plainer. The third-floor room (not accessible) was the only one to be provided with a fireplace; it also had an outward-facing window. The rooms on the first and second floors were lit by rather crudely constructed two-light windows with window seats overlooking the courtyard. Each room also had arrowslits in the outer walls to allow covering fire across the outer defences.

All of the upper rooms were entered from a spiral stair built into a thickening of the wall. The third-floor

A reconstruction of how the inner ward may have looked in the later fourteenth century. To the right, the entrance to the west tower is shown with its original first-floor entry, approached via an external wooden stair. This doorway was soon to be replaced with a ground-floor entry (Illustration by Chris Jones-Jenkins, 1992).

Above: *At the end of the east curtain wall, a pair of latrines — with their discharge shafts — were positioned dramatically above the edge of the river cliff.*

Right: *The toothing in the masonry — above the exterior of the arched doorway adjacent to the east tower — marks a distinct change in the direction of the cross-curtain wall.*

landing appears to have been developed into an angular battlement overlooking the east curtain wall. Above this there may have been a look-out turret reached by an outside stair.

Access to the second-floor wall-walk of the east curtain wall is from the spiral stairs. The wall-walk overlooks the almost precipitous side of the valley. It must have been easier to defend than the west wall-walk and is, consequently, a much simpler affair. The end of the curtain wall is broken, but a pair of latrine shafts at this point shows that it was always intended to end the wall in a spur at the edge of the cliff. There is a splendid view of

the Teifi valley from the wall-walk, and here you can appreciate the almost impregnable position of this side of the castle. The layout of the domestic buildings of the inner ward is also clear from this vantage point.

Now, continue down the spiral stairs to the courtyard. The ground-floor room of the east tower is entered from the courtyard through a round-headed door. This room, lit only by narrow slots on either side of the doorway, apparently had no direct access to the upper room except, possibly, by ladder. Traces of plaster, which originally covered all internal walls of the tower, can be seen in this room.

The arched doorway adjacent to the east tower was built at the same time as the tower itself, and in order to give access to the inner castle ditch. The doorway was protected by a portcullis, worked from the wall-walk above. Only a small section of this part of the cross-curtain wall was built to the original plan. Outside the doorway, look up and you will see the toothing from a wall running at right angles embedded in the masonry. The change in direction of the cross-curtain wall at this point suggests that the major part of the wall and the west tower were only added after there had been a significant rethink of the castle's layout.

Rear Defences

The courtyard was enclosed on the north-east and north-west sides by further curtain walls. They probably belong to a later phase of building. That on the north-east side, overlooking the river, is more slightly built than the others. A fragment of its wall-walk can be seen 10 feet (3m) above the courtyard. The remains of an earlier wall, possibly part of the defences of the preceding ringwork castle, stand just outside, on the edge of the cliff. The north-west curtain wall still stands to wall-walk level. It is pierced by another sally port leading out on to the Plysgog valley.

The north tower, facing the navigable stretch of the river, stands at the junction of the two curtain walls. It was built in the late fourteenth century when there were fears of rebellion in Wales, as well as the possibility of a French landing. It is clear that the tower was built across the end of the earlier north-west curtain wall and that it projected beyond in an angular bow. A long section of cliff in this area has collapsed at some time and has taken with it the northern part of the tower. Little of the tower now remains above ground-floor level.

A flight of steps from courtyard level leads down to a rock-floored inner room, and beyond that there is another small room at a lower level.

Domestic Buildings in the Courtyard

The low walls in the courtyard belong to various buildings which were ranged around the outer sides. The range of buildings alongside the north-east curtain wall appear to have been built at the same period as the north tower, and, to judge from remnants of the door jambs which survive, were of similar architectural quality.

There seems to have been a substantial building against the north-west curtain, which may have had a hall on the first floor. The rock-cut drains (no longer visible) found during excavation at

A view of the rear defences from the top of the east curtain wall. In the distance are the stumps of the north tower which projected out above the river cliff.

the northern end suggest a kitchen in this area. The limekiln at the other end — used for the production of mortar — is evidently later. At the south-west corner, next to the inner gatehouse, is a low wall belonging to a period earlier than the gatehouse; it is laid at a different angle and its stones were set in clay.

Right: *The low walls along the north-west curtain wall represent domestic buildings ranged around the outer sides of the courtyard.*

THE BOROUGH OF CILGERRAN

By the early thirteenth century a small town had developed outside the castle walls at Cilgerran. It was first mentioned in records in 1204, but there may have been an earlier settlement associated with the pre-medieval church site further west. The town, or borough, covered a similar area to the core of the present village, and had a weekly market in Castle Square. In the medieval period Cilgerran was noted for its fishing, particularly salmon. The salmon weir, located below the castle, had six traps and was, according to George Owen, writing in 1603, 'the greatest weir of all Wales'.

Fishing was important to the medieval economy of Cilgerran and the river Teifi was noted for its salmon. This manuscript illustration of a leaping salmon is from a thirteenth-century work of Gerald of Wales (d. 1223), who in 1188 had journeyed along the Teifi and marvelled at the river's wonders (British Library, Royal Ms. 13 B VIII, f. 23).

A HISTORY OF ST DOGMAELS ABBEY

St Dogmaels is situated a mile (1.6km) west of Cardigan, on the opposite bank of the Teifi, near the river's estuary. The abbey nestles in a pastoral bowl of open fields divided by a small stream which comes tumbling down from a steep and narrow valley on its short, frantic journey to join the Teifi.

In fact, the bowl of fields probably represents the original monastic precinct. Today it is surrounded by housing and other later development, thereby preserving the shape and separateness of the ancient religious community.

To the earliest monks, this spot — close to a natural spring — must have seemed to be an ideal place for devotion and contemplation. It was an oasis partly enclosed by tree-clad hills to the south and west, protected by the river Teifi to the north, and hidden from the estuary by a bend in the river.

The site takes its name from Dogmael, one of the early Christian saints whose influence continued to be felt in this area until the coming of the Normans. The abbey itself was a Norman foundation but there are strong indications that it lay on or near the ancient pre-Conquest church of Llandudoch. An early charter states that the Anglo-Norman lord of Cemais, Robert fitz Martin (d. 1159), gave 'the ancient church of

The eagle of St John, carved on a stone corbel from the north transept of the abbey church.

St Dogfael with possession of the land adjoining the same church, the name of which is Landodog' (*Llandudoch* in modern Welsh). The medieval abbey was to survive until its dissolution during the reign of King Henry VIII in 1536.

ST DOGMAEL AND THE EARLY CHRISTIAN CHURCH

St Dogmael (or Dogfael) is believed to have lived in the sixth century, but almost nothing is known about him save that he is supposed to have been the son of Ithel ap Ceredig ap Cunedda Wledig. He would thus have been descended from the fifth-century British prince and founder of the royal family of Gwynedd. Dogmael was also reputed to have been a cousin of St David. Judging from churches bearing his name, St Dogmael's influence seems to have been mostly confined to the Preseli area, although there are also dedications to him in Anglesey and Brittany.

Even less is known of 'the ancient church of St Dogfael', but from the rich collection of early Christian stones which has survived at or near the site of the later abbey, and from references in the Welsh *Chronicle of the Princes (Brut y Tywysogyon)*, it appears to have been an early monastery or *clas* church. During excavations of the Norman abbey, an early Christian stone was found under a wall of the chapter house, thus helping to substantiate the notion that the medieval abbey was built on or near the site of the ancient establishment. More recently, an archaeological ('geophysical') survey of the grounds has identified what appears to be a very early curving bank to the south of the claustral buildings. Such a bank may have defined part of the precinct of the early monastery.

By the sixth century a number of early Christian monasteries had become firmly established in Wales; St Dogmael's church at Llandudoch may have been one of them. Indeed, a medieval reference to the privilege of *nawdd* ('Noddfa Degwel'), or sanctuary,

Best appreciated from above, the Tironian abbey of St Dogmaels lies amidst a bowl of fields, close to the Teifi estuary (Skyscan Balloon Photography, for Cadw: Welsh Historic Monuments).

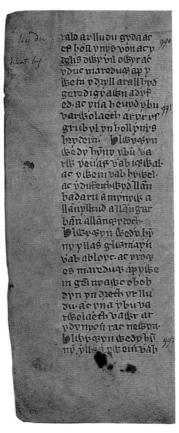

Although little is known of the 'ancient church of St Dogfael', Brut y Tywysogyon records the ravage of Llandudoch (St Dogmaels) by the Vikings in 988 (National Library of Wales, Peniarth Ms. 20).

THE TWELFTH-CENTURY NORMAN FOUNDATION

The remains of buildings that can be seen on the site today belong to the monastery founded early in the twelfth century by Robert fitz Martin, the Anglo-Norman lord of Cemais. Cemais included a large part of the Preseli area and was at that period somewhat insecurely held by the fitz Martin family from their castle at Nevern.

To the Anglo-Normans the pre-Conquest monasteries of Wales, with their strange customs and hereditary monks, epitomized all the defects which the newly reformed French orders had been created to put right. It is not surprising, therefore, to find Robert fitz Martin, within a few years of succeeding to his lordship, replacing the ancient monastery of *Llandudoch* with a community drawn from one of the new orders. In order to accomplish this, Robert had first to visit the mother abbey of Tiron (Eure-et-Loir) in northern France. He did this in 1113, returning with thirteen monks and a prior and was thus able to found a priory at St Dogmaels, presumably on the site of the old monastery. Five years later he visited Tiron once again, and came back with another thirteen monks and with permission to raise the priory to the status of an abbey. At about the same time, a small priory of Benedictine monks was founded two miles (3.2km) away on the opposite bank of the Teifi at Cardigan.

St Dogmaels appears to have been formally established as an abbey on 10 September 1120, with the enthronement of Fulchard as the first abbot, by the bishop of St Davids. It remained a daughter house of Tiron, subject to the jurisdiction of the mother house, with the ties between the two clearly defined. Every three years, the abbot of St Dogmaels had to make a hazardous journey across the English channel to Tiron at the feast of Pentecost, 'for the sake of strengthening and confirming our religion and of visiting the brethren'. St Dogmaels was frequently mentioned over the years in the cartulary of the abbey of Tiron, proving that it continued to owe its allegiance to the mother house at least until the beginning of the sixteenth century and probably up until its dissolution in the 1530s.

at St Dogmaels probably reflects the earlier importance of this monastery. Another early monastery or *clas* church with associated early Christian stones lies just a few miles away at Nevern. Monasteries were a notable feature of the early church, and later they were to emerge as the mother churches of Wales. Each contained a community or *clas* under an abbot. By the late eleventh century clerical marriage was accepted in the Welsh church and as a result the property rights of the *claswyr* were often transmitted from generation to generation.

In 988, according to the Welsh chronicles, the Vikings attacked Llandudoch, along with other monastic churches near the Welsh coast, including St Davids, Llanbadarn, Llancarfan and Llantwit Major.

The Anglo-Norman monastic communities at St Dogmaels, and here at Benedictine Cardigan, were isolated for much of the twelfth and early thirteenth centuries. The site of Cardigan Priory is now occupied by the parish church.

During the early years of the abbey's history, its monks must often have felt isolated and nervous, for this was a tempestuous period. Territory on both banks of the Teifi was constantly changing hands, as first one side and then the other gained the upper hand. In 1136, for instance, Robert fitz Martin and his fellow Normans were spectacularly defeated at the battle of Crug Mawr near Cardigan. They were forced to retreat southwards, leaving most of the area once again in the hands of the Welsh princes. Two years later the abbey itself was attacked, not for the first time, by Scandinavian pirates. And in 1165, as if to remind the monks of St Dogmaels of their isolation, the Lord Rhys (d. 1197) of Deheubarth expelled the Anglo-Norman monks from the neighbouring priory of Cardigan.

Despite the wars, construction of the new abbey continued throughout much of the twelfth century. The nave of the abbey church, however, does not seem to have been finished in this earliest phase of construction. Nevertheless, the claustral buildings were sufficiently complete by 1188 for Gerald of Wales to stay there with Baldwin, archbishop of Canterbury (1184–90),

The abbey buildings were sufficiently complete by 1188 to accommodate Gerald of Wales — shown here in this manuscript illustration — and the archbishop of Canterbury on their preaching tour through Wales (Syndics of Cambridge University Library, Ms. Ff. 1. 27, f. 1v).

A reconstruction of how St Dogmaels Abbey may have looked in the later Middle Ages. The abbey is seen from the south-west with the cloister in the foreground and the abbey church beyond. The infirmary lies to the top right (Illustration by Chris Jones-Jenkins, 1992; with modifications, 2000).

on their preaching tour of Wales, gathering support for the Third Crusade. In his *Itinerary Through Wales* describing the tour, Gerald wrote 'we slept that night in the monastery of St Dogmael, where, as well as on the next day at Aberteifi [Cardigan], we were handsomely entertained by prince Rhys'. It is clear from this account that the monks were on good terms with the Welsh prince.

A few years later, in 1191, there was further fighting in the area as the Welsh under Rhys swept across Cemais and captured the castle at Nevern forcing Robert fitz Martin's son, William, to abandon his stronghold in favour of a new site at Newport. It is not clear whether St Dogmaels was spared in the war.

The next we hear of the abbey is in connection with the questionable election of its abbot to the bishopric of St Davids. The vacancy for a new bishop occurred in 1198

on the death of Peter de Leia. Initially, both Gerald of Wales and Walter, abbot of St Dogmaels, were included in the list of candidates. Walter was completely unfitted for the responsibility for, according to Gerald, he could neither read nor write. Both were rejected by the archbishop of Canterbury who disliked Gerald and who, in any case, preferred to have an English monk in the post. Despite this setback Gerald was elected bishop by the cathedral chapter in June the following year. The archbishop of Canterbury was furious at the chapter's defiant attitude and in December he had Walter of St Dogmaels elected as bishop, so resulting in a double election which would ensure that both candidates lost their eligibility. The dispute went to the pope and after a number of visits to Rome by Welsh and English clerics to argue the case the pope quashed the elections of both Gerald and Walter.

THE THIRTEENTH AND FOURTEENTH CENTURIES

The middle years of the thirteenth century seem to have been a period of relative prosperity for the abbey. This may have been connected with a firmer English control of the area and the rebuilding of Cardigan Castle in stone in 1240. Much building and reconstruction were carried on at the abbey. The church was completed during this time, albeit to a modified layout, and the cloister was rebuilt.

In 1246 King Henry III gave a gift of 20 marks to the abbot and convent of St Dogmaels 'for the fabric of their church'. Towards the end of the century, in 1291, the value of the abbey was assessed as £58 11s. 4d., showing it to be a medium-sized institution by Welsh standards. Poor Cardigan Priory was worth only about £16 at the time.

All was not well, however, for within a few years the abbey was running into financial difficulties. These may have been due to a programme of extensive rebuilding necessitated by damage caused during the troubled times of the Edwardian conquest of Wales. In 1296, the abbot petitioned King Edward I that as 'they are much ruined and impoverished by the war which has been in their country ... that they may be allowed to have the help of a lady who wishes to make a covenant to them of 11 shillings worth of rent in the town of Cardigan'. Then, in 1317, the abbot complained about an excessive assessment of clerical taxes on his land, and a year later that poverty made it impossible for him to pay his taxes. The abbot and convent even went as far as appropriating the church of Maenclochog without permission and then had to obtain King Edward II's pardon. But St Dogmaels was not alone in its troubles, for in 1322 Cardigan Priory went into debt and had to be taken into royal custody.

It is possible that the abbey had difficulty in recruiting monks and, as with most other monasteries in Wales at this period, numbers were probably dwindling. Worse was to come. This was the plague known as the Black Death. It struck St Dogmaels in 1349 and, as we know from the diocesan registers, reduced still further the number of monks. The monastery never really recovered from the effects of the plague, declining population, and a generally growing disillusionment with the call of the monastic life.

By the turn of the century St Dogmaels was spiritually in a poor state. In 1402, a visitation by the bishop of St Davids revealed that there were only four monks (including the abbot) at the house. Licentiousness, it seems, was rife. Following an admonition by the bishop there was a gradual improvement. A century later, in 1504, there was a further visitation. This time the abbey was said to be in good order, the ruined chancel had been restored and there were six regular monks in addition to the abbot. The reference to the restoration of the chancel may also refer to the elaborate rebuilding of the north transept, which must have taken place at about this time.

At times during the later Middle Ages, the spirituality at St Dogmaels was not all it might have been and a visitation by the bishop of St Davids in 1402 revealed that licentiousness was rife. This early fourteenth-century manuscript shows a monk suffering for his misdemeanours (British Library, Royal Ms. 10 E IV, f. 187).

This common seal of the abbey dates from 1534, just two years before the monastery was suppressed along with hundreds of other religious houses throughout England and Wales (Public Record Office, E 25/40).

THE DISSOLUTION AND LATER HISTORY OF THE ABBEY

D espite the undoubted improvement, the monastic life at St Dogmaels remained a pale reflection of that to which the early monks had aspired. The end came in 1536 when, along with hundreds of other houses throughout England and Wales with an annual income of less than £200, the abbey was suppressed by King Henry VIII. The abbot and his eight monks had already acknowledged the king's supremacy in 1534 and no attempt was made to stem the tide of change. The assessed annual value of the monastery at the dissolution was £87 8s. 6d., and its rentals and tithes were assessed in 1537 to be £140 8s. 8 1/2d.

The major part of the abbey's possessions, including Caldey and Fishguard (p. 34), were leased to John Bradshaw of Presteigne, in Radnorshire. A few years later, in 1543, Bradshaw was able to purchase the properties

By the time that Samuel and Nathaniel Buck produced this view of St Dogmaels from the north-west in 1740, the abbey church and buildings had become ruinous.

This watercolour by John 'Warwick' Smith (1749–1831) shows the north transept in 1792, seen from the parish churchyard (National Library of Wales, PB 6326).

which he already had on lease. He built a mansion for himself, probably within the abbey precinct, and no doubt used stone from the abbey buildings for its construction. Subsequently, Bradshaw's mansion was allowed to fall into decay and today no remains of it are visible unless the later alterations and additions at the end of the west range belong to that building. Bradshaw was excused from keeping the chancel in repair, possibly because it had already been stripped of its lead. At the beginning of the seventeenth century George Owen described it as a ruin. In 1646 the site was bought by David Parry of Neuadd-Trefawr, near Cardigan, but neither he nor his descendants appear to have lived there.

The blocking of the nave at its western end to form a vestibule (p. 37) suggests that this part of the abbey church was later altered for parochial use. If so, it must have replaced the existing parish church of St Thomas the Apostle which stood on the opposite side of the stream, at the corner of Shingrug and David Street. According to witnesses in a dispute, the old parish church was still in use during the first half of the seventeenth century. It is unlikely, therefore, that the alterations to the monastic nave could have been made earlier than about 1640. The north transept is divided from the rest of the abbey church by the base of a late wall, suggesting that it was walled off for use as a private chapel, perhaps for the same family that might have earlier paid for its elaborate rebuilding in the sixteenth century.

Early in the eighteenth century, a new parish church was erected alongside the old abbey church. A century later, in 1847, this was replaced by the church which now stands on the site. Finally, in 1866, the vicarage and its coach house, were built with materials from the old abbey buildings.

In 1934 the remains of the abbey were placed in State guardianship by the Representative Body of the Church in Wales. The site was cleared and the masonry consolidated between 1947 and 1968 and the ruins are now maintained by Cadw: Welsh Historic Monuments.

THE MONASTIC LIFE

The monks of Tiron attempted to order their lives according to a strict interpretation of the Rule of St Benedict. *The sixth-century saint is seen here in a thirteenth-century fresco at Subiaco in Italy, holding a copy of his* Rule, *which was probably written between A.D. 535 and 550 (Scala, Florence).*

THE MONKS OF TIRON

By the later part of the eleventh century, a growing dissatisfaction was being felt in France with the regime of existing monasteries in that country. As a result of slackness and negligence and a too comfortable way of living, the Benedictine and Cluniac monasteries had lost much of the essential spirit of the *Rule* of their sixth-century founding father, St Benedict. In a search for a life of greater austerity and simplicity many monks left the greater abbeys, seeking out instead wild and deserted places, and living the lives of hermits. One such group of hermits went to live in the forest of Craon near the eastern borders of Brittany. Amongst them was Bernard (d. 1117), a monk who had previously been at the abbey of St Cyprian, near Poitiers.

After being sought out by the monks of his old abbey, Bernard retired to an even more remote and deserted hermitage at Chaussey on the Normandy coast. Later he returned to St Cyprian to become its abbot, but the life did not suit him and before long he left the monastery again to return to his hermitage. At his hermitage Bernard gathered around him a group of followers. Together with his disciples, in 1109 he established a new monastery at Nogent, in the diocese of Chartres. There, the monks attempted to return to a strict interpretation of the *Rule* of St Benedict in the ordering of their daily lives. Five years later the abbey moved to Tiron.

Bernard was, according to his biographer (himself a monk of Tiron), not only a generous and humble man who had undergone many hardships, but also an influential preacher. Bernard's reputation for holiness attracted attention and brought the new monastery to the notice of those in power. Soon, groups were sent out from Tiron to establish new colonies, each one comprising twelve monks headed by a prior. Regular assemblies, attended by representatives of each daughter foundation, were held at Tiron so that the purity of the new order's discipline could be maintained. St Bernard of Abbeville, as he later became known, died in 1117 at the age of seventy-one.

Tiron's influence in Britain was limited. St Dogmaels was the only Tironian abbey to be established in Wales or England, although the house also had daughter priories in Wales and Ireland. A few Tironian abbeys were established in Scotland, but they soon formed their own independent order.

EVERYDAY LIFE

A key feature of the Tironian congregation was an insistence that the monks themselves should be skilled craftsmen such as carvers, joiners, smiths, and painters. Nevertheless, much of their time was taken up with prayer and their days were organized around a series of services in the abbey church. And, as with monks in other monasteries, they were expected to keep the rule of silence. At first the Tironian monk's habit was light grey in colour; later it was changed to black.

Although initially the monks came from France, novices were, no doubt, soon recruited locally. Indeed, St Dogmaels may have been one of the first Norman abbeys to recruit Welshmen who in an earlier age might have found a calling in one of the *clas* churches.

The monastic vows laid great stress on poverty, chastity and obedience, and these ideals were characteristic of the monastic life, especially in the early years. To these three virtues might be added that of charity, for the abbey would have taken in any pilgrims and travellers requiring hospitality and perhaps occasionally the poor and the sick as well. Later, an abbey might become a place of retirement for previous incumbents and those who could afford to purchase annuities.

As well as prayer and manual work, study was also an important part of a monk's life. St Dogmaels had its own library. One of its books, a thirteenth-century copy of Eusebius's *Historia Ecclesiastica*, has survived and is now in the library of St John's College, Cambridge. In an age when few could read or write outside the church, a community such as a monastery often became important as a cultural centre. This seems to have been the case with St Dogmaels. Long after it had ceased to be a monastery, it was remembered nostalgically by the poet Sion Mawddwy as the place where

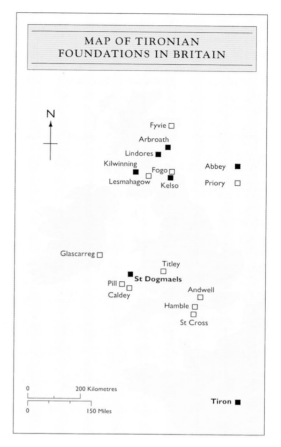

MAP OF TIRONIAN FOUNDATIONS IN BRITAIN

N

Fyvie □
Arbroath ■
Lindores ■
Kilwinning
Fogo □   Abbey ■
Lesmahagow
Kelso ■   Priory □

Glascarreg □
Titley □
Pill □ □   ■ St Dogmaels
Caldey   Andwell □
Hamble □ □
St Cross

0   200 Kilometres
0   150 Miles

Tiron ■

Study was important within the Tironian monastic life. In this fifteenth-century manuscript detail, two monks share a book (British Library, Additional Ms. 18192, f. 110).

Among the books in the abbey library at St Dogmaels was this thirteenth-century copy of Eusebius's Historia Ecclesiastica, *now at St John's College, Cambridge (Master and Fellows, St John's College, Cambridge, Ms. A. 5).*

the silver harp of Henllys had traditionally been delivered for safe keeping.

Not all aspects of the monastic life at St Dogmaels were to continue to flourish, however, and in later centuries the abbey suffered from a decline in standards as well as in its financial position. In 1402, for instance, at the time of the visitation by the bishop of St Davids, there appears to have been considerable deterioration. Due to pestilence and neglect, the number of monks had been reduced to four, but they were consuming food for a much larger number. One of the monks, a certain Howel Lange, had been found drunk and was ordered to desist from drinking wine and *meddyglyn* (the Welsh form of mead) for a year 'on account of his excess and his evil deeds'. Evidently, the monks had also been drinking in taverns in St Dogmaels and Cardigan. Moreover, they had been consorting with women, while ordinary people had been allowed to wander in and out of the cloister. The bishop commanded that all these practices be stopped and that none of the monks and lay brothers be allowed outside the monastery without special permission.

THE ECONOMY OF ST DOGMAELS ABBEY

Originally, in a Tironian abbey, the monks themselves did all the work associated with running the monastery. In later years, however, much of the manual work at St Dogmaels would have been done by lay brothers. Lay brothers were not expected to take part in the rigorous pattern of services except on Sundays and major feast days. As well as working in the abbey precinct the lay brothers would be found on the extensive estates which the abbey owned. By the thirteenth century the abbey owned more than 700 acres (283ha) of arable land in Pembrokeshire alone. Much of this land had been acquired by gift.

The abbey's greatest benefactor was its founder Robert fitz Martin. He had generously endowed it with rights of chapelries and with lands in St Dogmaels and Mynachlog-ddu in the lordship of Cemais, as well as Cockington and the rich manor of Rattery in Devon. Robert's wife Matilda gave land at Moylgrove and his mother, Geva, gave the island of Pyr, or Caldey, near Tenby. During the thirteenth century William of Cantinton gave land at Fishguard, including a water-mill, to the abbey. In addition tenements were acquired in Haverfordwest and Pembroke and half a burgage in London.

The gift of Ynys Byr, or Caldey, by Geva is interesting because this was the site of another early monastery. The monastery became a dependent priory of St Dogmaels and was rebuilt around a small cloister garth. Primitive, but extensive, remains of the buildings, including the diminutive church, have survived. In the late twelfth century two other priories were established and then granted to St Dogmaels as dependencies. These were Pill Priory, founded by Adam de la Roche near Milford Haven, and Glascarreg Priory in County Wexford, Ireland. They were small monasteries, but

In this early fifteenth-century manuscript illustration, a monastic community, in the choir of their abbey church, sing a Requiem Mass. The Tironians originally wore a grey habit, though this was later changed to black (British Library, Additional Ms. 18192, f. 110).

Above left: *Caldey Island was given to St Dogmaels Abbey by the founder's mother, Geva. The early monastery already established on the island soon became a dependent priory of St Dogmaels and was rebuilt around a small cloister garth (Wales Tourist Board).*

Above right: *Pill Priory was probably founded about 1200, by Adam de Roche, as a dependency of St Dogmaels.*

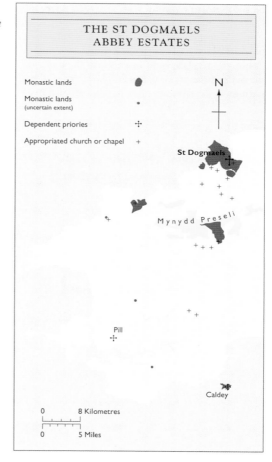

THE ST DOGMAELS ABBEY ESTATES

Monastic lands

Monastic lands (uncertain extent)

Dependent priories

Appropriated church or chapel

N

St Dogmaels

Mynydd Preseli

Pill

Caldey

0   8 Kilometres

0   5 Miles

each contributed pensions towards the support of the mother house.

In the early years, the economy of St Dogmaels was based on farming and livestock. It had hill granges on Mynydd Preseli suitable for sheep grazing and lowland granges for growing crops and wintering flocks. In addition the lowland granges had access to sea-fishing. In later years, with the decline of available labour and the probable disappearance of lay brothers following the Black Death, St Dogmaels needed to resort, like many similarly placed Cistercian abbeys, more and more to renting out property. Of particular importance to the abbey's economy were the rectorial tithes which had been gradually acquired over the years from a number of churches in Cemais and other parts of south-west Wales. By 1535 the value of tithes from appropriated churches and pensions from daughter priories amounted to almost two-thirds of the abbey's annual value.

THE DEVELOPMENT OF THE ABBEY BUILDINGS

THE NORMAN ABBEY

The earliest surviving remains at St Dogmaels date from the first half of the twelfth century. These include parts of the east and west ranges and substantial areas of the abbey church. The church, never very large by the standards of abbeys generally, ended up even smaller than originally planned. In the first phase, it appears that only sufficient of the church was built to fulfil the immediate needs of the monastery and that the western part, for use by the laity, was not finished.

The twelfth-century church was intended to be a cruciform building with an aisled nave, a short presbytery — probably with a central apse — and transepts with apsidal chapels. The lower parts of the side walls of the presbytery remain, although largely rebuilt later, as do the bases of the piers of the crossing tower. The south transept, with its distinctive apsidal chapel, can also be

clearly seen. The lower parts of the south aisle piers are still visible and the base of the outer wall of the south aisle has been found under the cloister garth, but there are no traces of the north arcade except the lowest part of the easternmost arch next to the crossing. This suggests that only the eastern end of the nave, including the space between the rood screen and the *pulpitum*, was completed together with the south aisle. It was necessary to build the outer wall of the nave in order to provide a backing for the cloister, which at that date probably had timber arcading.

REBUILDING IN THE LATER MIDDLE AGES

The nave was completed in the thirteenth century, though it was to have a simpler arrangement without aisles. The presbytery was extended with a square-ended sanctuary

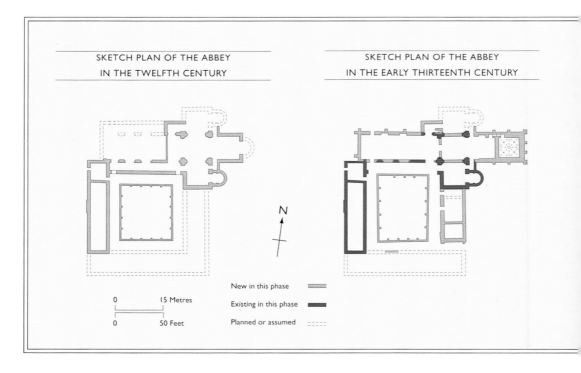

SKETCH PLAN OF THE ABBEY
IN THE TWELFTH CENTURY

SKETCH PLAN OF THE ABBEY
IN THE EARLY THIRTEENTH CENTURY

N

| 0 | 15 Metres |
| 0 | 50 Feet |

New in this phase

Existing in this phase

Planned or assumed

which was built, unusually for a Welsh church, over a vaulted crypt. About the middle of the century the cloister was enlarged northwards, with the north walk taking the place of the south aisle of the church. About the same time, the cloister arcades were rebuilt in stone.

The domestic quarters and cloister arcades were extensively rebuilt in the late thirteenth or early fourteenth century. To start with, a new infirmary was built as a separate building east of the complex. This was followed by a new chapter house at the rear of the east range. Evidently it was intended to reconstruct the whole of the east as well as the south range, for the inner wall of the chapter house is on the line of the eastern end of the rebuilt south range. The intervening section of the east range was not rebuilt, presumably for lack of money, and as a result is not aligned with chapter house and day room.

During the same period, the nave of the church was upgraded by inserting a new window in the west end and a new door and high-level window in the north wall. Later, either in the fourteenth or fifteenth century, much of the west range was altered to provide

improved accommodation for the abbot and a new wing was added for his guests.

The final alteration to the abbey church was the rebuilding of the north transept, with its elaborate stone-vaulted ceiling. The work took place in the early sixteenth century, not long before the suppression of the monastery. It was an unusual addition to a generally austere building, and its lavish design suggests it was intended as an individually distinct chapel, built perhaps as a memorial to the founder's family, the lords of Cemais.

LATER ALTERATIONS

After the dissolution the church was adapted for parochial use, with the west end of the nave being walled off to form a vestibule. During this period the north transept also appears to have been walled off suggesting that it may have been used as a private chapel. At the corner of the south and west ranges a new house was built, possibly for John Bradshaw (the new owner of the abbey) or his descendants.

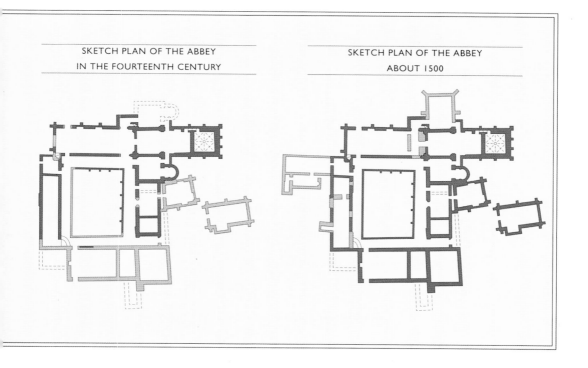

SKETCH PLAN OF THE ABBEY
IN THE FOURTEENTH CENTURY

SKETCH PLAN OF THE ABBEY
ABOUT 1500

A BIRD'S-EYE VIEW OF ST DOGMAELS ABBEY
FROM THE SOUTH

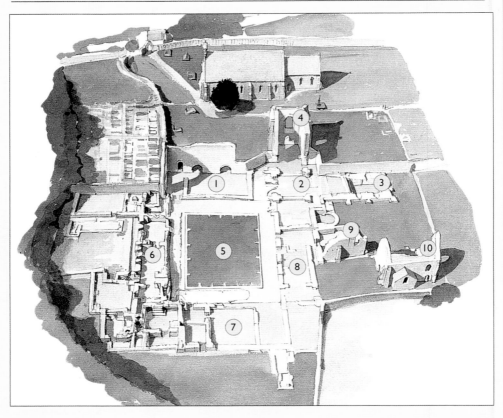

1 Nave — *eventually built to a modified plan in the thirteenth century, the nave lacked the usual west door due to its location set into the hillside. The monks would have entered through the south door from the cloister and non-monastic visitors through the north door, distinguished by its elaborate fourteenth-century ball-flower decoration (pp. 39–41).*

2 Monks' choir and crossing — *at the centre of the monastic church, this is where the Tironian monks attended their daily services. There was probably a tower above supported by the four great crossing arches (p. 41).*

3 Presbytery and crypt — *the high altar stood within the presbytery above a vaulted crypt. The crypt is unique among Welsh monastic churches and may have served as a repository for the relics of St Dogmael (pp. 41–2).*

4 North transept — *originally part of the twelfth-century church, this was entirely rebuilt in the early sixteenth century with a fine 'fan-vaulted' interior (pp. 42–4).*

5 Cloister — *the open square, or garth, was originally surrounded by four open passageways, or alleys (p. 44).*

6 West range — *the ground-floor room served as cellarage, with the upper floor providing accommodation for the abbot. The foundations at a higher level in the south-west corner represent a post-medieval house on the site (p. 45).*

7 South range — *the core of this range was the monks' dining hall. On the*

cloister side, there are the remains of the thirteenth-century laver, or washing basin, where the brothers washed before entering for meals (p. 45).

8 East range — *this was two storeys high with the monks' dormitory located on the upper floor (pp. 45–6).*

9 Chapter house — *originally contained within the width of the east range, but later extended so that the earlier room became a vestibule to the enlarged chapter house. The monks gathered here each day to hear a chapter of their Rule read aloud (p. 46).*

10 Infirmary — *built in stone in the late thirteenth century, the infirmary housed the sick and old members of the community (p. 46).*

(Illustration by Terry Ball)

A TOUR OF
ST DOGMAELS ABBEY

This tour begins at the west end of the abbey church, progressing along the nave towards the presbytery and the crypt, and then moving to the transepts. From the south transept the route continues around the cloister in an anti-clockwise direction, starting with the outer parlour and the west range, and looking at the remains of the other principal monastic buildings. The tour ends with the infirmary block on the east side of the abbey complex.

THE CHURCH

Standing at the west end of the church, below the large window, you can look eastwards, down the length of the church, without any interruption save for a few low walls. Originally, the view would have been broken by various screens and walls dividing the church into its constituent parts based on the way in which the building was used. In addition, the church was, to judge from the many fragments discovered during excavation, full of monuments of various types including canopied tombs, slabs and effigies.

From this point, the nearest low wall which you see is a late addition. It was probably introduced in the seventeenth century to provide an entrance

vestibule when the nave was used as a parish church.

The Nave

The church is somewhat unusual in not having a west doorway. The fact that the slope of the ground becomes much steeper at this end, giving little room, may provide the explanation. Instead, there appear to have been doors situated in the side walls at either end of the later vestibule.

The south door would have been entered from the cloister. Near it, in the corner, you will see steps built into the wall. These were a later insertion, and may have given access

A detail of the fourteenth-century ball-flower decoration around the north door of the abbey church.

direct to the abbot's house, or to the roof space above the nave. The north door would have been the main entrance for non-monastic visitors to the church. Seen from the parish churchyard side, it is a handsome doorway constructed in hard grey sandstone. The elaborate mouldings and ball-flower decoration indicate that it was rebuilt in the first half of the fourteenth century. The great west window has now lost all of its tracery but retains some of its mouldings at high level, suggesting that it also belongs to the fourteenth century.

Although the nave was laid out in the twelfth century, it does not seem to have been completed until the following century and by then certain changes had been made to the plan. The most obvious change was the abandonment of the intended aisles on either side of the nave. The nave was also lengthened slightly by moving the west wall a few feet further outwards. The remains of the piers of the south aisle arcade can be seen embedded in the south wall. The base of the outer wall was found during excavations beneath the cloister walk but is not now visible. The intervening spaces between the piers were filled up when the rest of the nave was completed to the new plan.

The thirteenth-century north wall of the nave stands almost to its full height. Apart from a four-light window set high up at the eastern end

A view along the nave of the abbey church, looking towards the east end. The surviving floor tiles in the nave probably date from the fifteenth century.

there were no windows in the north wall, presumably because of the height of the adjacent churchyard. There are two arched tomb recesses at the base of the wall.

The surviving floor tiles probably date from the fifteenth century. Originally the nave was paved with stone flags. The base of a wall near the eastern end of the nave marks the position of the rood screen. An altar, flanked on either side by doorways, would have been set against the west face of this wall. Steps from a central doorway in the screen date from later alterations when the nave was used as a parish church.

At the centre of the abbey church, four great piers supported the tower. Here, part of the twelfth-century north-west pier can be seen behind the remains of the pulpitum *— a large stone screen added in the thirteenth century to separate the nave from the east end of the church. The steps would have led to the top of the* pulpitum.

The Crossing and the Monks' Choir

At the end of the nave, the low walls between the two great western piers of the crossing represent the remains of the thirteenth-century *pulpitum*. This would have been a large stone screen separating the nave from the east end of the church. There was a central doorway through the screen, flanked by two small altars on the nave side. Masonry was later added in front of the *pulpitum*, possibly to strengthen it. The top of the *pulpitum* was reached by a spiral stairs next to the north-west crossing pier.

The four huge central piers were built to support a tower above the crossing. They belong to the twelfth-century church, and relate to a floor level which was some nine inches (22cm) lower than

the later tiled floor. Double attached shafts can be seen on the inside faces of the piers, situated below the position of the east and west crossing arches. Some of the scallop capitals belonging to these shafts were discovered during excavation. Other capitals found featured small sculpted heads.

The whole of the crossing area was occupied by the monks' choir. The choir stalls backed on to solid blocking walls to the north and south. Only the base of the wall between the south piers has survived; the thinner wall under the north arch is a later replacement. The broken grave slab in the centre of the choir floor was recorded in the sixteenth century as being that of the founder of the abbey. At the eastern end of the choir are slate slabs covering two further graves and a square floor socket for placing a lectern.

The Presbytery and the Crypt

Further to the east is the presbytery, within which stood the high altar. The eastern end of the presbytery was 2 feet (60cm) above the level of the crossing and was

A detail of one of the attached shafts in the crypt which helped to carry the vaulted roof.

reached by steps. Beneath this was situated a vaulted crypt, a unique feature amongst Welsh monastic houses.

A set of narrow steps on the north side of the presbytery leads down to the crypt, which appears to have been added in the thirteenth century, possibly as a repository for relics of St Dogmael. It is a square room with very thick walls, and was lit by narrow windows on three sides. The side walls contain a series of small holes for candle brackets. The crypt was covered by a vaulted roof, arranged in four bays each consisting of a four-part vault, supported centrally on a small pier which has been lost. The curved ribs of the vaults sprang out from this pier and were carried over to attached shafts situated in the corners and in the centre of each side wall.

The Transepts

The south transept belongs to the original twelfth-century church. Although almost ruined to ground level, it is distinguished by an apsidal chapel on the east side. The chapel was later blocked off. The opening between the transept and the south-east pier of the crossing, which may at first have led to an aisle, later gave access to an angled passage which permitted communication between the transept and presbytery. The choir stalls and screen wall under the crossing would otherwise have prevented such movement.

The most impressive surviving section of the abbey church is the north transept. It perhaps stood out just as

impressively when it was rebuilt in the early sixteenth century. The three outer walls of the transept still stand to roof height and are supported by massive buttresses, best seen from the parish churchyard. There was a large four-light window in the north wall and three-light windows in the side walls; all have lost their mullions and tracery.

Overhead there was a fine two-bay rib-vaulted ceiling of stone. The elaborate pendants of the vaulting and the corbels from which they sprang can be seen in the outer angles and on the centre of the west wall. The corbels are carved with figures of an angel (north-east), a lion (north-west) and the Archangel Michael (west, centre). A corbel from one of the crossing piers and bosses from the vaulting were found

A reconstruction of the east end of the abbey church, cut away to reveal some of the details of the vaulted crypt below the presbytery (Illustration by Chris Jones-Jenkins, 1992).

The substantial remains of the north transept, rebuilt in the early sixteenth century, still contain indications of the elaborate vaulted ceiling that sprang from elegant pendants supported by carved corbels.

during excavations. There is the base of a small altar in the centre of the east wall and two tomb recesses near the north-east corner.

As in the south transept, another angled passage gave access between the main transept space and the presbytery. There was, however, a tiny chapel set in this area, with an arched recess for a piscina set in the east wall.

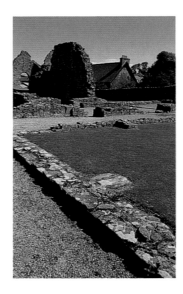

Below: *A reconstruction of how the north transept may have looked, just before the dissolution of the abbey (Illustration by Chris Jones-Jenkins, 1992).*

Left: *Surrounding the cloister garth, four passageways or alleys were covered with lean-to roofs. The bases which supported the arcade columns facing the garth can still be seen.*

THE CLOISTER

Returning over the crossing area, and leaving the church by way of the opening on the west side of the south transept, you will arrive in the north walk of the cloister. In the original scheme for the abbey church, this walk would have formed the south aisle of the nave, that is until the cloister was enlarged in the thirteenth century. The large rectangle of grass in the centre was the cloister garth or court. As at many other monasteries, this open space may have been used as a herb garden.

Surrounding the garth are the cloister alleys or walkways, each originally covered with a lean-to roof supported on an open arcade. The bases for the arcade columns, which supported pointed arches, can be seen projecting from the low walls of the walks. Many of the columns, which comprised either separate twin shafts or double shafts joined together by a stone web, together with their capitals, were found during excavations. The cloister walks were the heart of monastic life and besides giving access to the domestic buildings each traditionally had a specific use, such as studying in the north walk, washing in the south walk, and training novices in the west walk.

THE WEST RANGE

The lower floor of the west range dates from the twelfth century and is the best preserved section of the claustral buildings. At its northern end, adjoining the church, is the outer parlour, a square room where monks were permitted to meet visitors. Steps lead up to the outer door on the west side, while beyond are the low walls of the guest house added in the fourteenth or fifteenth century. The main ground-floor room of the west range was used as cellarage for food storage, and was lit by a series of narrow window openings in the outer wall.

A slight projection in the outer wall marks the position of the fireplace of the abbot's hall which would have been on the now destroyed floor above. The abbot's bed chamber and private chapel would have been above the outer parlour and accessible to the church via the spiral stairs seen at the end of the nave. The south end of the west range was extensively altered at a later date, probably to improve accommodation for the abbot and his guests. The large curved steps at the corner of the cloister date from these alterations. Later, the stairs behind the curved steps were blocked in, and a new stair turret was added on the opposite side of the range.

THE SOUTH RANGE

The doorway in the south range near the curved steps was the entrance to the monks' refectory. To the left of the door are two thirteenth-century red sandstone jambs. These are the remains of the laver, or washing-trough, where the brethren washed their hands before entering the dining hall. The rest of the range was rebuilt in the

The monks' dining room was located in the south range. The jambs of the thirteenth-century stone trough, or laver, where the monks washed before entering the dining room can still be seen. The trough was blocked in the later Middle Ages.

fourteenth century. The kitchen was probably at the angle where the south and west ranges meet.

All evidence of the kitchen was, however, destroyed by the post-monastic rebuilding in this area. Among the remains you will observe on the higher ground are three prominent circular ovens and the formal stairs belonging to a later house on the site.

The room at the eastern end of the dining hall was probably the warming-house, the only room in the abbey, apart from the infirmary and kitchen, where fires were allowed from November to Good Friday.

THE EAST RANGE

The east range was two storeys high. On the ground floor, the room at the corner next to the warming-house would have been the day room, an undercroft used for study and manual work.

The west range looking towards the north end, where the outer parlour was situated. This was the room where monks were allowed to meet visitors. Originally, the ground floor of the west range was probably used for storage with the abbot's private lodgings situated on the floor above.

The chapter house, probably rebuilt in the early fourteenth century, was one of the most important rooms in the abbey. The monks assembled here to hear a chapter of the Rule *read out.*

would have given direct access into the south transept of the church. The dormitory would also have been accessible from a day stair, reached from the cloister walk. At the southern end there was a latrine block, the ground-floor outlet of which is now marked by the slate slab over the stream near the warming-house.

THE INFIRMARY

The infirmary was built in the late thirteenth century as a separate building for the old or sick members of the community. It is located some way from the east range, away from the distractions of the cloister, and is entered through a pointed doorway on the west side. Its east and west gables still stand almost to full height while above the south wall can be seen the lower part of a barrel-vault roof which would have been slightly pointed at its apex. There is a vaulted recess on the south side.

Next there was a slype, or passage, leading out of the cloister to the infirmary. The room beyond may have been the parlour where talking was allowed for limited periods.

Halfway along the east cloister walk a wide opening, with ribbed, semicircular slate jamb bases on either side, leads into the vestibule of the chapter house. Originally the vestibule itself would have been used as the chapter house. The chapter house was one of the most important rooms in the abbey and, when funds permitted, it was rebuilt on a more elaborate scale at the rear of the east range. Every morning the monks assembled in the chapter house to hear a chapter of their *Rule* read out; it was here, too, that corporate business was discussed and discipline maintained.

Finally, wedged between the vestibule and the south transept, a door led to another small room (see ground plan), possibly the sacristy where vessels and robes for services were kept.

The first floor of the east range was given over to the monks' dormitory. At the northern end a night stair

The abbey infirmary, for the old and the sick members of the monastery, was built as a separate building some way from the east range.

THE ST DOGMAELS STONES

Several carved stones of mainly pre-Norman date have been found within the precincts of St Dogmaels Abbey or nearby. Some of these are grave-markers carved with commemorative inscriptions or ring-crosses. Others, also carved with a ring-cross, may represent boundary stones, perhaps used for marking the sanctuary area of the early Christian monastery. The twelfth-century stones may be connected with the Tironian abbey. The monuments below are in roughly chronological order and dates given are approximate only.

I A tall stone pillar with incised inscriptions in both Latin (on the face) and Old Irish ogam (on the left-hand edge). Ogam is an alphabet with each letter represented by one or more notches or strokes arranged in relation to a vertical line. Both inscriptions indicate that the stone marked the grave 'of Sagranus, son of Cunotamus', possibly a local chieftain of Irish descent. This was the first bilingual Latin/ogam inscription identified in Wales. In the nearby parish church, at west end. Fifth or sixth century (Nash-Williams 384)

2 Part of an upright slab carved with a Maltese cross in a circle with a long stem and spirals. It may represent a liturgical fan and may be compared with similar carvings in Ireland. Eight or ninth century (Nash-Williams 385)

3 The lower part of a similar slab (now inverted) carved with the stem of a cross and spirals. In nearby parish church, near pulpit. Eight or ninth century (Nash-Williams 386)

4 A pillar carved with a ring-cross and bosses reminiscent of metalwork attachments. Discovered under the wall of the chapter house during excavations in 1949. Eight or ninth century

5 An incomplete slab with a rounded top, skilfully carved with a Maltese cross in a circle. In nearby parish church, near south door. Eighth or ninth century? (Nash-Williams 388)

6 Part of a slab carved with a Maltese cross in a circle. Below is a standing figure with arms outstretched in prayer. Found in 1921 near Bryngwyn Farm, 1/2 mile (0.8km) south of the abbey. Now on display in the National Museum & Gallery, Cardiff. Eighth or ninth century (Nash-Williams 130)

Stone number 6, found at Bryngwyn Farm (National Museums & Galleries of Wales).

7 A pillar carved with a ring-cross in outline, similar in form to some freestanding crosses. Found in 1996 near Bryngwyn Farm, about 1/2 mile (0.8km) south of the abbey. Now on display in the National Museum & Gallery, Cardiff. Eighth or ninth century

8 Part of a pillar with a fragmentary cross with a distorted ring, or a shield, carved with the letters D and I. Twelfth century? (Nash-Williams 387)

9 A pillar, one face of which is roughly carved with irregular decoration, including what appears to be a shield with crosses and circles. Originally found at Pant Tirion Farm, 1 1/2 miles (2.4km) north-west of the abbey, and later moved to Manian-fawr Farm before being brought to the abbey in 1906. The holes indicate reuse as a gate-post. Twelfth century? (Nash-Williams 389)

Stone number 4, discovered under the chapter house during excavations in 1949.

PENTRE IFAN AND CARREG COETAN ARTHUR BURIAL CHAMBERS

The south-western part of Wales is rich in prehistoric sites, providing some of the earliest archaeological evidence for human activity in the region. The sites range, for example, from caves which have revealed evidence for occupation during the Palaeolithic, through to flint-chipping floors of the Mesolithic, and on to the often dramatic remains of stone burial chambers set up over 5,000 years ago during the Neolithic period.

On the northern side of the Pembrokeshire peninsula, it is the huge stone (megalithic) burial chambers of the Neolithic period which predominate. They frequently stand out as massive megalithic tombs, and are often known in Wales as *cromlechau*. In this area their distribution is concentrated in and near the lush valley of the Nyfer river. The group includes Pentre Ifan and Carreg Coetan Arthur, both of which are in the care of Cadw: Welsh Historic Monuments. Elsewhere in the region, other Neolithic tombs and monuments lie on the southern side of Mynydd Preseli, and further west along the coastal fringe between Fishguard and St Davids.

Although the tombs vary in detail, each generally consists of a burial chamber formed by a massive capstone supported on a number of upright stone slabs. The entire edifice may then have been hidden beneath an earthen mound or stone cairn (*carn* in Welsh), though none of the covering mounds has survived in this area. Modern methods of dating — especially radiocarbon dating — suggest that the megalithic tombs found in this part of Wales, along with their counterparts elsewhere in Britain, belong to Europe's earliest known architectural tradition.

In contrast to the tombs, the houses of the Neolithic living are much more elusive and far less imposing. A settlement site is known at Clegyr Boia near St Davids, but the huts were built largely of wood and have left few remains.

Left: The dramatic profile of Pentre Ifan burial chamber creates the illusion that the massive capstone is almost floating above the tall slender upright stones.

THE NEOLITHIC PERIOD AND THE SPREAD OF NEW IDEAS

The Neolithic period, as identified by archaeologists, appears to emerge hesitantly in Britain around 4000 B.C., when domestic agriculture was introduced from Europe after having slowly spread across the Continent. Until that time, people had survived essentially as hunters and gatherers: mobile groups living on game, fish and wild plants. The gradual change from hunting to farming resulted in a widespread transformation of the landscape as the natural forest was, little by little, cleared in order to grow crops. These changes meant that people were eventually able to follow a more settled pattern of life.

The introduction of agriculture undoubtedly brought with it an increasing emphasis upon land, and perhaps the development of rights of territory and inheritance. In this context, the traditional rights of a kindred or tribal group to an area of land may well have been reinforced by the overt presence of its ancestors. And it is possible that this presence was visibly symbolized by the megalithic tombs, and made manifest by ceremonies which no doubt took place from time to time at the entrances to the chambers. Used over many centuries then, the tombs are perhaps best interpreted as family vaults. For the communities whose not inconsiderable efforts they represent — and whose ancestral bones they contained — such prominent structures could have represented stability and continuity within a now more permanently settled landscape.

Apart from the significance of the tombs themselves, it is important for us to appreciate that the adoption of settled farming methods was a complicated process and depended on the spread of agricultural knowledge and the movement of ideas and people from one area to another. During the earlier part of the Neolithic

An artist's impression of a Neolithic farming settlement around 4000 B.C. Much of what is shown is conjectural, based on scant evidence recovered in Britain and Europe (National Museums & Galleries of Wales).

period much of inland Wales would have been still covered in dense forest, making safe and easy travel difficult. Consequently, transport was often waterborne and people travelled using rivers and the sea.

Jutting out into the Celtic Sea between the Bristol Channel and Cardigan Bay, the Pembrokeshire region was well placed to take advantage of any seaborne traffic. It is not surprising, therefore, to find that many of the prehistoric sites in the area are near to, or within sight of, the sea. In the course of time, the region came to share with other lands around the Celtic and Irish Seas many aspects of their cultures and ways of life.

By around 2500 B.C. there appears to have been a marked decline in the use of megalithic burial chambers. During the ensuing Bronze Age, through to about 1500 B.C., different kinds of ritual and ceremonial monuments seem to have assumed greater importance. Typical of this period were stone circles and henges which began to appear across the landscape of Britain.

There are no identified henges in this part of south Wales, but two stone circles are known: Gors Fawr, at Mynachlog-ddu, and Meini Gwyr, near Llangolman, both on the south-eastern side of Mynydd Preseli. Gors Fawr is the better preserved of the two. It contains sixteen stones,

none more than 4 feet (1.2m) high, arranged in a circle with two stone outliers. Meini Gwyr is embanked and only two of its stones remain. Although small by the standards of circles elsewhere, the significance of these two circles lies in the fact that both are situated almost within a stone's throw of Carn Menyn, an outcrop of dolerite rock which was the source of the famous 'blue' stones used in the remodelling of Stonehenge about 2100 B.C.

MEGALITHIC MONUMENTS OF THE NYFER VALLEY

There are remains of half a dozen Neolithic tombs in the Nyfer valley, or close by on the northern slopes of Mynydd Preseli. Local names suggest that originally there may have been others in the area, but all material evidence of these has now disappeared. Most of the burial chambers in the group are located within sight of the sea; indeed, four of them lie within a mile (1.6km) of the coast.

Of the Nyfer group of tombs the nearest to the sea is Carreg Coetan Arthur, which lies on the outskirts of Newport on the south side of the Nyfer estuary. This is a well-preserved cromlech, dating from about 3500 B.C., with a polygonal chamber. To the west of Newport, just to the north of the main road, is Cerrig y Gof, an unusual group of five small rectangular chambers arranged in a circle; the capstones remain on four of the five chambers, but have slipped from their original positions.

There are two tombs on the north side of the Nyfer. The nearest, Trelyffant, has two parallel chambers, but only one of the chambers retains its capstone. Llech y Drybedd lies in a field south-west of Moylgrove, and is another well-preserved polygonal cromlech. There are two more tombs in the northern foothills of Mynydd Preseli. Pentre Ifan, with its enormous capstone and curved facade of standing stones, is one of the finest megalithic monuments in Britain. Bedd-yr-afanc, near Brynberian, contains a long, narrow passage, giving it a somewhat different character from the other tombs in the area. Another Neolithic cromlech lies at the eastern end of Mynydd Preseli, at Mountain near Crymych, near the head of the pass into the Cleddau valley.

The design and construction of Neolithic tombs vary considerably from region to region. Most of the burial chambers in the Nyfer valley group, however, belong to the type known as portal dolmens, a name derived from the way in which the entrance to the tomb is framed by two large stone slabs. In the closely related type of tomb known as a court cairn, each side of the entrance is flanked by a curved facade of tall stones to form an uncovered court. Both portal dolmens and court cairns are restricted in their geographical distribution to Ireland and the western peninsulas of England, Scotland and Wales, suggesting that the type evolved in the Irish Sea region out of a megalithic tradition which itself originated in continental Europe.

Here, as elsewhere, the burial chambers were probably intended for the interment of members of the community over a long period. The tombs may have been left open initially to allow for repeated access, in which case the portal stones would have been visually significant in accentuating the entrance. Burials may also have been accompanied by some form of funeral rite in front of the entrance. This may account for the elaborate and imposing forecourt facade of standing stones which survives at Pentre Ifan and, albeit in a very ruined condition, at Carn Turne on the south-western slopes of Mynydd Preseli, near Wolf's Castle.

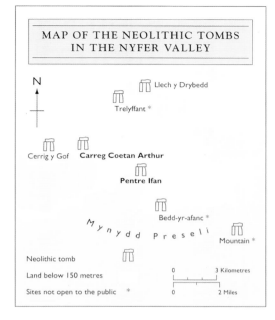

MAP OF THE NEOLITHIC TOMBS IN THE NYFER VALLEY

N

Llech y Drybedd

Trelyffant *

Cerrig y Gof   **Carreg Coetan Arthur**

Pentre Ifan

Bedd-yr-afanc *

M y n y d d   P r e s e l i

Mountain *

Neolithic tomb

Land below 150 metres

Sites not open to the public   *

0   3 Kilometres

0   2 Miles

Cerrig y Gof — another of the Nyfer valley tombs — is an unusual group of five separate burial chambers arranged in a circle.

Llech y Drybedd is another well-preserved polygonal burial chamber built in the portal dolmen tradition.

PENTRE IFAN
BURIAL CHAMBER

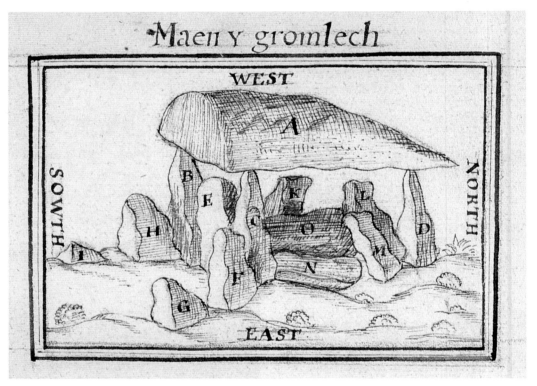

The earliest known illustrative record of Pentre Ifan appears in George Owen's manuscript, Description of Penbrockshire in Generall, 1603. Owen's careful description shows that although some of the stones have since fallen, Pentre Ifan looks very much as it did four hundred years ago (British Library, Harleian Ms. 6250, f. 97).

INTRODUCTION

Overlooking the estuary of the Nyfer, Pentre Ifan burial chamber lies amid a patchwork of small fields divided by hedgebanks on the northern slopes of Mynydd Preseli. Approaching the remains of the tomb along the narrow footpath, you will see its massive but shapely capstone resting almost precariously on the points of three unusually tall supporting stones. It is this eye-catching appearance which has helped to make it one of the best-known examples of an early Neolithic tomb in Britain.

The tomb has long been known to antiquaries and was the first monument in Wales to be afforded protection under the Ancient Monuments Protection Act of 1882. As long ago as 1603, George Owen of Henllys (d. 1613) included Pentre Ifan, or Maen y gromlech as he called it, in his famous *Description of Penbrockshire in Generall*, saying that it was 'soe highe, that a man, on horsbacke, may well ride under it'. Owen's careful description of the cromlech is interesting because it shows that, although some stones have since fallen, the monument is generally of much the same appearance today as it was nearly four hundred years ago. Since then, Pentre Ifan has been described and illustrated by many topographical writers and painters.

DESCRIPTION

Pentre Ifan is basically a portal dolmen type of tomb constructed with unshaped, but carefully selected, slabs of the local igneous rock. The formal 'entrance' to the tomb is at the up-slope or southern end. It comprises two tall portal stones erected parallel to each other with a slightly lower blocking stone set between them at right angles to form an 'H' on plan. The spaces between the blocking stone and the portal stones were filled with dry-stone walling, parts of which can still be seen. In theory, at least, the blocking stone was intended to be movable so that the chamber behind it could be opened up as required for additional burials. In the case of Pentre Ifan it is doubtful if this could have happened without dislodging one of the main portal stones. Access to the chamber was, in fact, probably gained from the side.

The burial chamber is roughly rectangular in shape and has a level floor dug into the slope of the site. At the northern end there is a single large pointed stone forming part of the structure. Originally there were other large stones, but not of full height, forming the sides of the chamber. The gaps between these stones may have been filled by dry-stone walling. In Owen's day four of the side stones remained, but now all have disappeared except for one fallen on the north-west side. Two other stones, which may once have been standing, lie adjacent to the chamber.

The two portal stones and the end stone support an enormous capstone, almost 17 feet (5.1m) long, and 8 feet (2.4m) above the chamber. The capstone, which weighs over 16 tons, is thickest at the southern end and tapers towards the northern end; it also slopes downwards towards the northern, thinner end. The visually unexpected arrangement of the capstone, which appears to float and contradict the laws of gravity, taken together with the delicate way in which the capstone rests on the pointed ends of the supporting stones, gives the monument an illusion of instability.

At the southern end of the tomb, on either side of the portal stones, are remains of a crescent-shaped facade of tall stones. Two of these stones survive in position on the east side. On the west side, the remains of a broken stone

and a restored stone stump show the line of the facade. When complete the facade stones would have formed a partially enclosed court which was probably used for performing ceremonies in front of the tomb's entrance. The curved facade is similar to those found at court cairns in Ireland. However, in the Irish monuments the burial chamber itself is usually covered by a number of separate corbelled stones rather than by a single massive capstone. In all, Pentre Ifan seems to combine features from both the portal dolmen and the court cairn varieties of tomb. It perhaps suggests that the site represented a cultural fusion of the different types, or maybe that the tomb was built in two separate phases, with the facade being added at a later date to an already existing portal dolmen. On the other hand, the Pentre Ifan community may simply have been seeking to differentiate itself from neighbouring groups.

Behind and on either side of the burial chamber are traces of a slightly raised mound. This has been partly reconstructed to give an impression of the great cairn of stones which

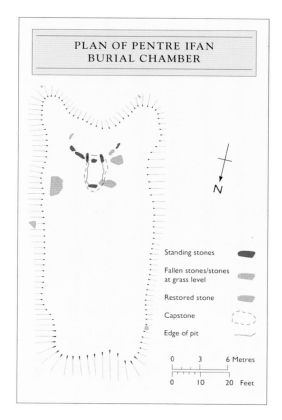

PLAN OF PENTRE IFAN BURIAL CHAMBER

N

Standing stones

Fallen stones/stones at grass level

Restored stone

Capstone

Edge of pit

0   3   6 Metres

0   10   20 Feet

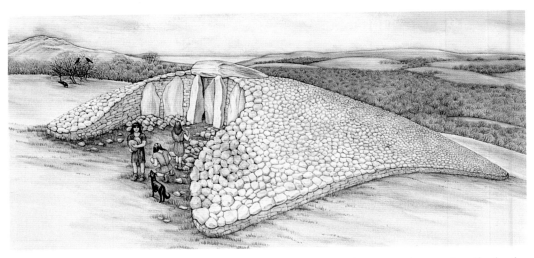

An artist's impression of how Pentre Ifan may have looked with a great cairn of stones tapering away from the chamber (Illustration by Jane Durrant, 2000).

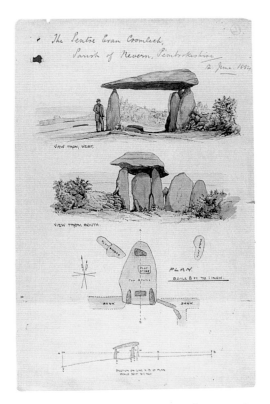

Pentre Ifan was the first site in Wales to be protected under the Ancient Monuments Protection Act of 1882, and in 1884 General Pitt Rivers — the first Inspector of Ancient Monuments — visited the burial chamber with his assistant, W. Tomkin. This page from their notebook shows field sketches and a plan of Pentre Ifan by W. Tomkin; General Pitt Rivers can be seen acting as a scale.

formed a tapered hillock around the burial chamber about 120 feet (36m) long and extending forward to frame the forecourt at the southern end. It is impossible to know whether the cairn simply rose to the same height as the capstone, leaving that exposed, or whether the cairn actually covered the capstone so that only the facade and portal stones remained visible like an opening into a cave.

EXCAVATIONS

The tomb was excavated in 1936–37 and again in 1958–59 in connection with the consolidation of the monument. Very few objects were found during the work, and no traces of burials had survived. Apart from some flints, the most important finds were a few fragments of pottery discovered inside the chamber and in the forecourt area. The excavations revealed a number of small holes running in two lines down each side of the tomb. One hole still retained a small upright stone and it is possible that originally stones in these holes marked the edge of the cairn and helped to support it. On the eastern edge of the 'cairn' two small pits were found; these were filled with stones and may have been used in some kind of ceremony associated with building the tomb, or with burying members of the community within it.

CARREG COETAN ARTHUR BURIAL CHAMBER

Carreg Coetan Arthur — this small compact burial chamber is similar to other tombs in the Nyfer valley and appears to date from about 3500 B.C.

The small size of this compact burial chamber makes it more typical a member than Pentre Ifan of the group of Neolithic tombs which clusters around the Nyfer valley. It is the most coastal of the group, lying as it does near the very edge of the estuary, overlooking the sheltered waters of Newport Bay, a good landing point for the boats of the first farming settlers with their seed corn and domestic animals. One might think, therefore, that this tomb could have been one of the earliest of the group, with later tombs being built as the settlements spread further up the valley. But it is the only tomb that has produced any dating evidence from excavations on the site, and the hypothesis must therefore remain unproven. The radiocarbon dating of the burnt wood from cremations in the tomb show that it was built around 3500 B.C., fairly late in the spread of Neolithic cultures within Wales as a whole.

The tomb is composed of four large upright stones forming the sides of the burial chamber, two of which support the wedge-shaped capstone. All five stones are local erratics, carefully selected for their size and shape, but apparently unfashioned and with no marks or tooling to be seen. The

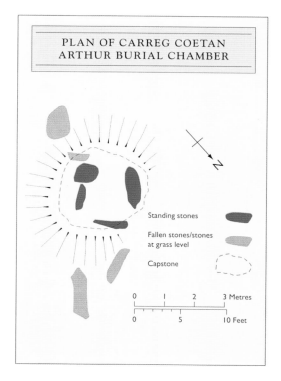

PLAN OF CARREG COETAN ARTHUR BURIAL CHAMBER

Standing stones

Fallen stones/stones at grass level

Capstone

| 0 | 1 | 2 | 3 Metres |
| 0 | | 5 | 10 Feet |

side of the tomb away from the sea has the distinct feel of a blocked door, as the thicker, higher side of the capstone has beneath it a large flat 'portal' stone, similar to that at the front of Pentre Ifan. The practical entrance to the tomb must have been through the gaps between the sidestones either on the west or south-east of the chamber.

Archaeological excavations at Carreg Coetan Arthur have shown that the tomb was once surrounded by a small cairn or mound, composed of the local subsoil of sandy glacial drift. The cairn was revetted by a ring, or kerb, of boulders about 36 feet (11m) in diameter. Only a section of the base of this cairn survived, but presumably it once at least partially covered the tomb, concealing the interior of the chamber and sealing the entrances.

The chamber itself was considerably disturbed, but the small intact part of the surrounding mound showed that the cairn material had been placed on a surface carefully laid with small slabs of stone, upon which had been placed large round-bottomed bowls of a coarse black pottery. These bowls had contained the cremated bones of several adult humans. Scattered around the chamber were found many fragments of hard brown pottery vessels, similarly round-bottomed, but which had been 'burnished' or polished to give a shiny effect to the surface. Several hollows of unknown, but presumably religious function connected with the burial rites, were found near the chamber. These were filled with charcoal, and in one case with part of a polished stone axe.

The 'coetan' part of the name of the tomb refers to the old game of quoits, and is often associated with Neolithic burial chambers in England and Wales. In this particular case, King Arthur — who frequently appears in the place-names of historic sites — is supposed to have played the game using the 'carreg' or great capstone of the tomb.

FURTHER READING

The author and Cadw would like to thank Professor R. R. Davies, Professor R. A. Griffiths, Frances Lynch-Llewellyn and Professor Sir Glanmor Williams for their comments during the preparation of the first edition of this guidebook, and Dr Nancy Edwards, Dr Mark Redknap and Dr D. M. Robinson for their assistance with this edition.

O. E. Craster, *Cilgerran Castle* (HMSO, London 1957); ninth impression (HMSO, Cardiff 1983).

R. R. Davies, *Conquest, Coexistence and Change: Wales 1063–1415* (Oxford 1987); reprinted in paperback as *The Age of Conquest: Wales 1063–1415* (Oxford 1991).

Thomas Jones (editor), *Brut y Tywysogyon (Chronicle of the Princes)*, Peniarth version (Cardiff 1952); Red Book of Hergest version (Cardiff 1955).

D. J. C. King, 'The Defence of Wales', *Archaeologia Cambrensis*, 126 (1977), 1–16.

J. R. Phillips, *History of Cilgerran* (London 1867).

Ian Soulsby, *The Towns of Medieval Wales* (Chichester 1983).

St Dogmaels Abbey

Janet Burton, *Monastic and Religious Orders in Britain 1000–1300* (Cambridge 1994).

F. G. Cowley, *The Monastic Order in South Wales 1066–1349* (Cardiff 1977).

E. M. Pritchard, *History of St Dogmael's Abbey* (London 1907).

C. A. Ralegh Radford, *St Dogmael's Abbey* (HMSO, London 1962); seventh impression (HMSO, London 1975).

Glanmor Williams, *The Welsh Church from Conquest to Reformation*, second edition (Cardiff 1976).

Pentre Ifan and Carreg Coetan Arthur Burial Chambers

W. F. Grimes, *Pentre Ifan Burial Chamber* (HMSO, London 1953).

W. F. Grimes, 'Pentre-Ifan Burial Chamber, Pembrokeshire', *Archaeologia Cambrensis*, 97 (1948), 3–23.

F. M. Lynch, 'Portal Dolmens in the Nevern Valley', in F. M. Lynch and C. Burgess, editors, *Prehistoric Man in Wales and the West* (Bath 1972).

Sian Rees, *A Guide to Ancient and Historic Wales: Dyfed* (London 1992).

Julian Thomas, *Rethinking the Neolithic* (Cambridge 1991).

R. C. Turner, 'Pentre Ifan Burial Chamber, Pembrokeshire: The Story of the First Ancient Monument in Wales', *Transactions of the Ancient Monuments Society*, 36 (1992), 99–118.